It's So Hard to Love You

Staying Sane When Your Loved One Is **Manipulative, Needy, Dishonest,** or Addicted

BILL KLATTE, MSW, LCSW

KATE THOMPSON

New Harbinger Publications, Inc.

Publisher's Note

This publication is designed to provide accurate and authoritative information in regard to the subject matter covered. It is sold with the understanding that the publisher is not engaged in rendering psychological, financial, legal, or other professional services. If expert assistance or counseling is needed, the services of a competent professional should be sought.

Distributed in Canada by Raincoast Books

Copyright © 2007 by Bill Klatte and Kate Thompson
              New Harbinger Publications, Inc.
              5674 Shattuck Avenue
              Oakland, CA 94609
              www.newharbinger.com

Cover design by Amy Shoup
Text design by Michele Waters-Kermes
Acquired by Melissa Kirk
Edited by Gail Saari

Printed in the United States of America

Library of Congress Cataloging-in-Publication Data

Klatte, Bill.
  It's so hard to love you : staying sane when your loved one is manipulative, needy, dishonest, or addicted / Bill Klatte and Kate Thompson.
    p. cm.
  ISBN-13: 978-1-57224-496-2
  ISBN-10: 1-57224-496-8
  1. Interpersonal relations. 2. Love-hate relationships. I. Thompson, Kate. II. Title.
HM1111.K565 2007
158.2--dc22
                     2007012999

09   08   07

10   9   8   7   6   5   4   3   2

This book is dedicated to our family: our mother, Jayne Klatte, and our brothers Richard Prestor and Owen Klatte, for your love, support, intelligence, sense of humor, and artistry. It's been quite a ride . . . and the ride continues.

Contents

Acknowledgments

Thanks first to you, Kate. I'm lucky to have you as my sister. This book would not have been possible without your partnership. We even wrote this book together without fighting (much). A testament to your patience! Thank you to my friend Joe Kelly. Your support and encouragement throughout the years has been invaluable to me. I am inspired by your commitment to making this planet a better place for children. Thank you, Joy DiNicola, for all the positive energy and kindness you have shown me over the years.

This book is better because of our Fuerstenau cousins: Karen, Vicki, Jeannie, and Steve. We've grown up together, and you've always been a consistent and essential part of my life. A special hello to my fantastic grandsons, Mason Holcombe and Aidan Holcombe. You guys rock!

—Bill Klatte

My first thanks go to you, Bill, for inviting me to join you in writing this book. It's been a delight and a challenge, and I'm so grateful we had a chance to do this. To my sons, Logan, Lucas, and Graham Schinbeckler—and all of my patchwork family, near and far—thank you for your love, encouragement, and practical suggestions. Dan, you are always here to illuminate my days and remind me why I do what I do.

For all sorts of other help, I wish to thank Mary Nelder, Susan Rheault, Beth Mastin, Fay Becks, and Peter Carter. I appreciate the time, energy, and enthusiasm you shared to help me iron out some of the wrinkles. Thank you, most of all, to the Creator, who brings so many teachers into my life, helping me see the need to let go with love—and then to learn how to do it.

—Kate Thompson

We both extend our thanks to our agent, Robin Dellabough of Lark Productions, and Melissa Kirk, our acquisitions editor at New Harbinger Publications, for your insightful help and determination to move this book forward.

—Bill and Kate

Introduction

Do you know someone who is hard to love? Do you get frustrated with that person at times? Maybe often? Are you feeling worried, afraid, angry, or sad? If so, *It's So Hard to Love You* can help. In this book you will learn that many people care about someone who does things that make him or her hard to love.

What you learn in this book can certainly help you deal with the annoying aunt who pushes her ideas on you, a hurtful teenager, or the best friend who won't stop talking about himself—those who are rude, inconsiderate, or overly needy. However, the primary purpose of *It's So Hard to Love You* is to help you handle beloved adults who are *really* irresponsible, frustrating, hateful, or even borderline criminal. You will learn how to stay sane, even when your problematic loved one has bewildering long-term problems. You'll have a chance to explore ideas and options to help yourself deal more happily with your difficult relative or friend.

Here are examples of situations you might be dealing with:

- Your adult daughter is living with a guy who takes her money and won't let her visit you.

- Your brother keeps getting fired from jobs and can't see that his own behavior is at least part of the problem.

- A longtime friend has called you yet again to borrow money for a weekend at the casino "just this once."

- Your sister has an eating disorder that truly frightens the family.

- Your spouse's lifelong friend tells lies and takes advantage of your whole family. Your spouse doesn't see it.

- Both your parents drink too much, and you're worried about them. And you don't like to admit it, but you're also worried you'll end up taking care of them if they lose everything because of their destructive habits.

- One of your adult sons has attention-deficit disorder and can be exhausting and frustrating to deal with. His presence in your home is making life very hard for the whole family.

- Your father gives you the silent treatment whenever you displease him.

- One of your grown children has physical or emotional problems that make it very difficult for her to handle adult responsibilities. You try to help, but nothing you do seems to make any difference.

These situations, and countless others like them, are daily realities for many people. In fact, you will find many possible variations within the pages of this book. More important, you'll find information, practical solutions, and support that will help you deal more successfully with a problematic loved one—no matter what his or her problems are.

Whether you find yourself trying frantically to help, or watching helplessly as they stumble and crash, these folks take a toll on everyone around them. At times, you might feel like you're going crazy. Well, your reactions are completely normal. Most people who care about a difficult friend or relative face similar problems, which can result in:

- Daily stress in the family

- Separation and divorce

- Damage to other relationships

- Financial difficulties

- Physical illness

- Emotional breakdown

- Forgetfulness

- Difficulty concentrating

- Depression

- Troublesome adult children returning home to live

- Involvement with police, lawyers, and the courts

LET GO WITH LOVE

We've found that many people respond in one of two ways when confronted with a loved one's damaging actions. One is to try to rescue the person, and the other is to give up in anger and frustration.

Letting go with love is the middle ground between those two responses. It's a third option that works in relationships with people who are hard to love. Letting go with love does not mean dropping completely out of someone's life at one extreme—or trying to make them do what you think they should at the other extreme.

Although your situation is probably complicated and unique in many ways, others who live with similar problems have improved their lives by learning to manage their problems in new ways. Our hope in writing this book is to help you learn the two aspects of letting go with love. They are:

1. You can accept difficult people without accepting their harmful behavior.

2. Taking care of yourself is a loving thing to do that also benefits others.

These principles for living are made up of several smaller ideas and steps that you can practice and learn. We have found them to be helpful and practical in our own lives and in the lives of those we work with.

The good news is that you can learn to let go with love, too. In *It's So Hard to Love You*, you'll find information, support, and exercises that show you how to understand what is currently going on and how to make changes.

You'll discover that no matter what factors surround your loved one's actions, and no matter what anyone says, *you* decide what is helpful and harmful for you. Even with people who have a disease or limiting condition beyond their control, *you* are the one who can and must decide what works for you and what doesn't. By following our suggestions, you can learn how to do that. Doing so will make it possible to find peace and contentment, even if your "crazy-making" friend or relative makes no changes at all.

At the back of the book, we've listed books and organizations that will help you learn more skills to improve your relationships. *It's So Hard to Love You* is just one step along the way—but we hope it's a helpful step. Thank you for letting us walk along with you for a while.

HOW TO USE THIS BOOK

We've written *It's So Hard to Love You* to be read from beginning to end, because the knowledge and skills in each chapter build on one another. You will find a number of self-assessments to enhance each chapter's content and to guide you.

We suggest you get a notebook or other journal to go along with this book. It could be an inexpensive spiral notebook or a nicely bound book made specifically for journaling. No matter what it looks like, make sure you feel comfortable using it. Some people like to decorate their journals with designs, stickers, or pictures they enjoy. If you use a computer, print out your entries and keep them in a three-ring binder—which you can also personalize.

As you work through the coming chapters, use your journal for the writing activities we suggest. It will also come in handy when you want to keep track of other reactions, questions, impressions, and ideas that come to mind as you read.

As you read this book and write in your journal, you'll discover that you interact with the world through actions, thoughts, and feelings. You can use those three elements to explore what's going on with yourself and your difficult friend or relative. Describe *what happened* (actions and events), *what you think* about what happened (thoughts), and *how you feel* about what happened (feelings).

You don't have to be a great writer to keep a journal. Spelling, grammar, and handwriting don't matter. Your journal is just that—yours. Whether your entries are short or long, it's a great place to let off steam, sort through problems, express gratitude, and so on. You can doodle or draw or paste in magazine pictures and photographs. It's not meant to be perfect. It is meant to be a helpful companion for you. One last suggestion about your journal: write the date at the beginning of every entry. Later on, you'll find it interesting and encouraging to look back and to see how much you've learned and grown!

SO, WHO ARE WE. . . ?

We, Bill Klatte and Kate Thompson, are brother and sister. We grew up in southern Wisconsin with two other brothers and a whole raft of cousins. Life was sometimes wonderful and sometimes not. The great times were punctuated by frequent moves, family struggles, and then our father's death when we were in our teens. Within a few more years, nearly all our other adult relatives had died as well. But led by the matriarch of the family, our mother, our extended family has hung together.

Our life paths continued to take us both into troubled relationships and other personal challenges. Those experiences also gave us many of the sweetest gifts life has to offer—personal growth, deep relationships, children and grandchildren, and satisfying work.

Our bond as brother and sister has deepened over the years, despite our living in different countries. Bill is a city boy, through and through, still living in a suburb of Milwaukee, Wisconsin, where we were born. Kate is an equally passionate country mouse who loves life on Manitoulin Island in northern Ontario, Canada. Our differences and similarities have blended together over the years to turn us into close friends and professional colleagues who have the unusual pleasure of also being siblings.

... AND WHY HAVE WE WRITTEN THIS BOOK?

For many years Bill counseled people who dealt with problematic loved ones—relatives or close friends who kept making the same damaging mistakes over and over. He often wished he could find a book that he and other professionals could share with their clients. His goal was to help clients deal more effectively with the challenges that troubled loved ones presented—while still keeping their own sanity.

One day, Bill realized that if he wanted such a book to exist, he'd have to write it himself. After some visioning and preliminary work, he started writing. He soon realized he needed a partner he trusted. The first person who came to mind was Kate. She had a great deal of experience counseling and teaching adults, and they had always shared a common understanding of what makes people tick and how to support them.

Through our own personal journeys and our work with others, we've learned many concepts and skills that have helped us live more contented lives. We've come to accept that we cannot change another person—even though we still sometimes wish we could. Letting go with love has worked so well for us and for the people we work with that we want to share this process with others. This book is the result of our decision to do that.

MOVING FORWARD

Join us on this challenging and interesting journey. You don't have to do magic. Just do your best, be as honest with yourself as you can be, and try our suggestions. We're confident you will find answers to some of the dilemmas you've wrestled with. So here we go ...

I

Troubled Lives

Linda was exhausted. Her twenty-eight-year-old son, Thomas, was on the rampage again. It hurt her to see him be so unkind to his daughter, and it scared her to be near his anger.

"I don't understand why you get so angry!" Linda cried. "I do everything I can to help you. Didn't I welcome you home again after you and Carla split up?" Linda slumped in the chair, weary tears sliding down her cheeks.

Thomas slammed his fist on the table. "What's the matter with you?! I just told you to babysit Jenny a few hours. Can't you even handle one little kid?"

"I know, Thomas, but she's just a little girl, and she gets messy. Children have to play. But you get so mad. I do everything to help you, Son. I don't know what else you think a mother should do. Just tell me, and I'll do it."

"Oh, for Christ's sake, Mom. Stop telling me how to raise my own kid. I know what Jenny needs. And I know what I need, and what I need is a minute or two of peace around here. I got enough problems with my boss on my case. I don't need you giving me grief, too."

"Please, Thomas. Keep your voice down. Jenny might hear you," Linda pleaded as Thomas stomped out of the room. Like so many times in the past few years, Linda couldn't decide whether to scream in fury or crawl in a hole and die of sadness. And as always, she was afraid—afraid for Jenny, afraid for Thomas, and afraid for herself.

Sighing, Linda got up and started on the dishes. Water and soapsuds splattered onto the floor and counter, punctuating her frustration and confusion. "I just wish I knew what happened to my sweet little boy. If only things could be like they were when he was young. What have I done wrong? I don't know why he treats people this way. When is this going to end?"

TROUBLESOME LOVED ONES

Have you ever felt the way Linda feels? Is there a person you love who treats you or others badly and makes the same serious mistakes over and over? If you answered yes to either of these questions, you are not alone. And you may be surprised to learn that your story doesn't have to end the way Linda's does. You don't have to face an unending future of uncertainty and frustration.

Thomas is what we call a "troublesome loved one." In this book, we refer to loved ones who have serious problems as troubled, troubling, or troublesome loved ones—TLOs for short. We also interchange these terms with others, such as difficult or problematic relatives and friends, crazy-makers, etc. All these phrases refer to people we define as "adult relatives or friends we love who repeatedly engage in behaviors that seriously harm themselves or others." They might be our sons, daughters, brothers, sisters, parents, husbands, wives, extended family members, or close friends.

Problematic relatives and friends get into bad relationships. Some are intellectually challenged. Some may gamble or misuse drugs or alcohol. They might overeat or undereat to the point where their health is affected. Others are frequently depressed, overly angry, controlling, indecisive, fearful, or socially inept. All of them conduct their lives in ways that negatively affect their decisions and their actions.

Let's take a closer look at what a difficult loved one looks like.

"Adult relatives or friends we love . . ."

Our difficult relatives and friends are people we care about a great deal. They are people in their late teens and older. They may or may not live with us. We might see them very frequently or very seldom, and in some cases we might not even be speaking to them. They're people we care deeply about and want in our lives in a healthy way.

". . .who repeatedly engage in. . ."

Troubled loved ones make the same kinds of mistakes over and over. They continually make destructive choices in spite of everyone's efforts to help them change. This is one of the hallmarks of TLOs—they don't seem to learn from their mistakes.

Children and young teenagers can be expected to repeat their mistakes as part of their natural growth and maturing process. That's how they learn. But the difficult loved ones we discuss here are adults. It seems like they should make sensible decisions, but they don't. And that's why we think of them as troubled and difficult.

People who are generally stable and healthy cope reasonably well with difficult life challenges. Difficult loved ones seem to create them.

". . .behaviors that seriously harm themselves or others."

Problematic relatives and friends do things that have very significant negative consequences for themselves and those around them. They often either argue or stay distant. They may waste money, abuse alcohol or other drugs, parent poorly, or ignore their own needs.

We are not talking here about an insensitive uncle who tells off-color jokes or an annoying mother-in-law who drops by without calling in advance. We're talking about truly troubled people who allow themselves to be used, take advantage of others, or make an unending number of other very damaging choices. It's often the repetitive nature of these poor choices that makes them so serious.

HOW DOES YOUR TROUBLED LOVED ONE TREAT YOU?

If you feel ignored or misused, you're not alone. For many people dealing with a TLO, the following experiences are typical. Ask yourself if you experience any of them.

- Getting an angry response even when you speak and act calmly and with the best of intentions

- Being blamed for what your relative or friend has done

- Having to put up with endless excuses

- Being ignored when you offer advice or state your needs

- Giving help, but not being appreciated for it

- Hearing your loved one speak glowingly of others who have done much less than you have

- Lending money or items which are then returned late, damaged, or not at all

- Rarely, if ever, being able to count on her to help you as you have helped her

Let's take a look at Carolyn's experience with her troubled daughter.

It's hard for me to admit that my own children treat me the way they do. As long as I do for them it's fine; but when I don't do for them, it's not fine. Sometimes my kids will be nasty and mean to me and pick on me. My daughter was sweet as pie to me yesterday because I said I'd babysit, but when I ask for something in return she says no. She doesn't realize it's hard for me to run after two grandchildren. Also, when I'm not around, my daughter goes places by herself; but if I am around, she makes me go with her. When I ask her to go to the store to help me carry groceries she says, "Why don't you get somebody else to do it?"

BEHAVIORS OF DIFFICULT LOVED ONES

Difficult loved ones are not defined by their size, gender, abilities, education, or income. They are defined by their actions. It's what they do—and don't do—that makes all the difference in how you feel about them. Even if they feel sorry or embarrassed about their actions, they're still hard to love when they seem unable or unwilling to change their damaging behaviors.

The following list notes some of the troubling behaviors of problematic people. As you read it, keep in mind that no one is likely to exhibit all of them, though most troubled people display at least one or two. Also remember that these are behaviors—they are not the sum total of who your loved one is. Many difficult people intend to be, and are, very loving and wonderful. It's when they aren't loving and wonderful that they can be so damaging.

Troublesome people often do the following:

`Break promises and don't complete tasks.` She leaves projects unfinished; is often late; fails to keep appointments and dates; doesn't make phone calls. Despite frequently not following through, she can't figure out why you're upset.

`Manipulate.` Trying to maintain some sense of control, this crazy-making person will twist circumstances and words to put others at a disadvantage. He might appear sad so you'll feel guilty, or get angry so you'll give in. He does things that upset you and then says you're being unreasonable. In the worst cases, these folks can make you doubt your own sanity.

`Lose their temper.` Lack of control leads many to blow up at home or in public, strike out physically, throw things, swear, and call others names. They are often irritable and blame someone else for their own unmanageable feelings and actions.

`Be critical or negative.` He complains about almost everything. He instantly and regularly points out what's wrong with people and situations.

Break the law. He may get frequent traffic tickets; lose his driver's license; pass bad checks; steal; get arrested for disorderly conduct or domestic violence. Again, it's common for him to blame the police, lawyers, you, the kids, or the court system for his woes.

Frequently quit jobs or get fired. It's not unusual for TLOs to quit school, get fired, or walk off the job. Conflicts with bosses, teachers, and coworkers are common.

Mismanage money and possessions. Some troubled relatives and friends have no idea how to manage money. Others won't spend a dollar, even for necessities, especially on anyone else. These individuals often don't look after the possessions they do own. They constantly struggle with unpaid bills and loans; unmanageable credit card debt; bankruptcy; car repossession; and other money problems. Their money problems are the result of impulsive actions or poor decisions on their part, not financial events beyond their control.

Refuse to plan or participate. This problematic loved one doesn't concern himself with planning for retirement, the children's education, or even daily events. Vacations and other special occasions may never happen, simply because he won't save for or discuss them.

Lie. Despite proof that the bank account is empty, a difficult person might deny she has spent all her money. Or she claims things are great at school or work—until you hear she's flunked out or been fired. The phone call to say she has to work late turns out to have been made from a bar or another man's apartment.

Move frequently. These moves are sometimes the result of a conscious decision to avoid creditors, the law, or "nosy" neighbors. At other times they are the result of the person's not feeling settled within himself. He rarely understands how difficult constant moving can be on the family.

Neglect or abuse children. An adult whose life is full of chaos may neglect her children's physical or emotional needs; abuse them; expose them to adult situations, such as drinking parties or sexual situations; leave them alone; or leave them with irresponsible caregivers.

Choose "bad" friends and partners. Whether a leader or a follower, a TLO might associate with someone she doesn't even like if she feels sorry for him, is afraid to say no, or hopes to get something from him. Some difficult loved ones stay in unhealthy relationships simply because they don't want to be alone.

Sabotage relationships. By exaggerating problems, spreading rumors, and telling different versions of a story to different people, a difficult loved one can make others so miserable they finally go away. He may belittle others, behave irresponsibly, or lie frequently. After all this, he wonders why people don't want to be with him.

Engage in risky behavior. The list of risky behaviors is almost endless, but it includes unprotected or indiscriminate sex; reckless driving; accepting dangerous dares; foolish financial schemes; carrying weapons; using or selling drugs.

Cut people out. They might refuse to talk to or even acknowledge people they have decided are "wrong." When they cut off family members, their coldness complicates and damages all relationships within the family. Communication becomes strained, and people end up taking sides. Family events become obstacle courses.

ANOTHER WAY TO LOOK AT DIFFICULT LOVED ONES

So far we've looked at specific things TLOs often do that make them hard to love. Now we mention specific groups that these troubling friends and relatives often fit into. Putting people into these groupings is admittedly an arbitrary process, but we do so to help you gain a little more insight into your troubled friend or relative. It's also important to point out that some members of these groups are not at all troublesome, as we define it in this book. They might be fully involved, loving, and contributing family members. These groups are:

- Substance abusers

- Activity abusers

- People with emotional problems and mental illnesses

- Individuals with developmental delays

- People with challenges such as fetal alcohol syndrome, learning disabilities, and attention-deficit/hyperactivity disorder

- Self-injurers

- Aggressors

- Physically dangerous persons

It can be difficult to fully understand troubled people, what they do, and why they do it. But since defining and understanding your TLO's behavior might help you deal with her, let's take a closer look at these groups that problematic people often fit into.

One additional point needs to be made here. Several of the groups we've discussed include individuals who have a condition resulting from an accident, illness, genetics, or problems at birth or in childhood. As a result, you might be more reluctant to see these people as troublesome because their troubles are not their "fault."

Take the example of an uncle who has lost his leg in a work accident. Now he drinks too much and has frequent anger outbursts, but his family finds it difficult to demand better behavior from him because of his accident and resulting physical disability. They put up with his drinking and anger because they feel sorry for him and believe they don't have a right to be mad at him.

Or what about the woman who experienced brain damage at birth, the man who got bounced from one foster home to another, or the person who has a terminal illness? How should you feel about these troubled people? It's not their fault life dished out these problems to them, is it? Don't they deserve extra patience and compassion?

Because these situations are sometimes so confusing, it may be helpful to step back for a moment and focus on a single concept: Concentrate you energies on yourself and how you deal with your TLO—not on your TLO's problems or how they came about. If your loved one's behaviors are a problem for you, you have a right to deal with them as such, regardless of why he does them. Patience and compassion are wonderful qualities, but taking care of yourself is a wonderful quality as well. Be sure to take care of yourself when a troublesome loved one makes life intolerable—whether it's his "fault" or not.

Substance Abusers

These TLOs drink alcohol or misuse other drugs. Whether they misuse their substance every day or only a few times a year, the important factor we look at in this book is the extent to which their misuse causes problems for themselves and those around them.

Substance abusers are often unable to stop once they start, and they frequently plan their days around their ability to get and consume their "fix." They frequently misuse despite the protesting or pleading of their families. These misusers keep on using even when they know it's causing serious problems in their lives—or is even killing them. Their substance becomes a trap that won't let go.

Substance abusers all have one trait in common: whether using or not, they have a different way of seeing themselves and the world than other people do, unless they get treatment. Even when people stop abusing their drug, they often remain argumentative, controlling, and distant if they don't get help.

Activity Abusers

Just like substance abusers, activity abusers participate in their habit for the relief or the rush it brings. These difficult people misuse gambling, sex, shopping, work, exercise, or other activities. Even if they don't partake often, they may compulsively misuse the activity over and over. In some cases, activity abusers give up everything in order to satisfy their emotional needs. Like substance abusers, activity abusers usually try to keep their problem a secret, but those closest to them almost always know the truth.

One unique problem with some of these activity abuses is that they can look socially acceptable, even admirable. This makes it even harder to recognize that there's a problem. It's difficult for outsiders to see that Uncle Henry's financial success and accumulated wealth belie a fractured family living with a workaholic. It would be hard for friends and acquaintances to know that Aunt Sally's ceaseless energy and thin body actually mean an obsession with working out and that her family feels frustrated and excluded.

Substance abusers and activity abusers have several traits in common. They usually:

- Use their substance or activity to avoid difficult thoughts, feelings, and situations

- Harm themselves and others physically, financially, and/ or emotionally with their excessive behavior

- Remain emotionally distant from those around them

- Become more dependent and more difficult as time goes on

- Suffer from more than one type of abusive behavior

- Need help to stop their misuse of the substance or activity

People with Emotional Problems and Mental Illness

Problems in this category range from manageable conditions to life-altering disabilities. Those who live with conditions such as depression, anxiety, or obsessive-compulsive disorders are often helped by counseling or medications.

People with Developmental Delays

These individuals have lower than average intelligence and are limited in various daily living skills such as communication, self-care, physical dexterity, academics, and/or work. Their limitations can vary from minor to profound. Individuals with developmental delays might have difficulty making effective decisions and expressing or channelling their emotions appropriately.

Jim and Sandi's son graduated from high school after taking all special education classes. He lived at home until his early twenties, but the stress he created profoundly affected their marriage and their other three children. They finally told him he had to move out. They helped him find an efficiency apartment and pay his bills. Sandi said this about her son:

> He constantly argued with us when he was home ... unless he was holed up in his bedroom, which is where he spent most of his time. He got fired from busing tables because he thought he was better than that. He'd get phone calls from strangers and send them money. If anybody was nice to him, he thought they liked him, when the truth was they were usually making fun of him or using him. We'd try to tell him, but he wouldn't listen. He'd listen to strangers before he'd listen to us.

People with Challenges such as FAS, LD, and ADHD

Many people have been diagnosed with disorders that are hard to categorize for our purposes here. Yet these conditions can challenge or overwhelm those who have them, as well as those who love the affected person. Three of these conditions are fetal alcohol syndrome or effect (FAS or FAE); learning disabilities (LD); and attention-deficit disorder or hyperactivity disorder (ADD or ADHD). They all range from moderate to profound, and they can certainly cause actions and attitudes that are hard to love.

Self-Injurers

People who harm themselves might have an eating disorder, or otherwise physically injure themselves. Common eating disorders are excessive overeating, anorexia nervosa, and bulimia. Overeating, undereating, or bingeing and purging all give the sufferer a feeling of having some control over their bodies when everything else feels out of control.

Self-injurers cut, scrape, burn their skin, or injure themselves in other ways. This self-injury is also an attempt to gain control over memories or experiences that feel too overwhelming to cope with.

Aggressors

Aggressors taunt, stalk, mistreat, or take advantage of others physically, sexually, emotionally, verbally, financially, or psychologically. Whether through a single incident or ongoing abuse, the harm they inflict can be severe. The aggressor might be aggressive toward anyone—spouse, children, other family members, friends, coworkers, or strangers.

Physically Dangerous Persons

Some difficult loved ones become dangerous. They might threaten or attempt suicide, or they might harm another person. In fact, domestic abuse is all too common and can involve anyone—young or old, female or male, gay or straight, married or single, physically disabled or not.

Take seriously any threats or attempts of physical harm. If you are aware of such a threat, talk with trusted relatives, friends, or professionals about it. Do not keep it to yourself.

You can call a help line if you have one in your community, or you can talk to a health professional. If your loved one has a probation officer, therapist, priest, or other professional, consider contacting them. If those people are unavailable, or you don't feel comfortable with them, call the police. Police officers have the authority to take someone into custody if the officer determines that she is a danger to herself or others.

It's understandable that you might be reluctant to call legal authorities, but remember that it is not your actions that lead to outside involvement. It is your loved one's choices and actions that cause the danger. By asking for help, you are taking reasonable precautions and acting wisely. If you are concerned about your safety, or the safety of others, you must act to protect yourself and them by calling attention to the situation as soon as possible.

HOW SERIOUS ARE MY TROUBLESOME LOVED ONE'S PROBLEMS?

After reading the information we've presented here and thinking about your own situation, you might be wondering what to do with it all. You've read about behaviors and conditions that apply to your situation, as well as some that don't. Perhaps some of the information brought up ideas and problems you hadn't even thought of or noticed before.

The following exercise will give you a chance to gauge the extent of your TLO's problems. This can be especially helpful if you aren't quite sure how bad things really are or if others tell you you're overreacting or underreacting. In any case, this scale will help you see if your views are on track and help you deal with your situation more confidently.

Consider asking your spouse or other concerned friend or relative who is not your TLO to complete the exercise, too. Afterwards, you can talk about it together, comparing your results and looking at new ways to think about the situation. Maybe you'll decide to work through this book together, as well.

Gauging the Extent of Your TLO's Problems

With your TLO in mind, read each statement below. Check a box to show whether you agree or disagree with the statement. If you're unsure about your response to a statement, go with your first instinct. If you have more than one troubling friend or relative, do this exercise separately for each of them.

My difficult loved one …	Agree	Disagree
1. Often loses his temper		
2. Often gets depressed		
3. Often becomes fearful or anxious		
4. Uses other people, or is used by them		
5. Intimidates others, or is easily intimidated by others		

My difficult loved one ...	Agree	Disagree
6. Constantly makes excuses or blames others for her problems		
7. Cannot say no to others, or won't take no for an answer		
8. Does not keep promises		
9. Frequently seeks reassurance from others		
10. Repeats the same harmful actions over and over		
11. Rarely or never admits a mistake		
12. Lies even after being confronted with clear evidence to the contrary		
13. Asks others to lie for him		
14. Stops communicating with others for various lengths of time		
15. Gets defensive when people try to talk about what she has done		
16. Has a mental or physical condition that limits her ability to be fully independent		
17. Abuses alcohol, illegal drugs, or prescription drugs		
18. Does not follow doctor's orders about his medical treatment		
19. Spends money foolishly or selfishly		
20. Gets involved with unhealthy partners or frequently changes partners		

21. Has children who are often out of control when with him		
22. Has an extremely disorganized or excessively clean home		
23. Has been fired from more than one job		
24. Has threatened or attempted suicide		
25. Has threatened to, or has, physically harmed another person		
26. Has spent time in jail or prison		
Totals		

Write the total number of check marks from the Agree column: _____.
This is your score.

SCORING

This quiz has a low score of 0 and a high score of 26. Use the following rating to get some indication of the extent of your friend or relative's problems. Keep in mind these ratings are indications only.

0-3 Points → Low. Your loved one may have problems, but he generally functions quite well and is usually seen by others as doing okay. If he's in his late teens or early twenties, it's possible that some of his struggles are age-related. He may "grow out of" some of these behaviors and attitudes.

4-6 Points → Medium. Your problematic person's behavior sometimes interferes with her ability to make healthy and effective decisions. The results of her poor decisions may show up at home, on the job, at school, or in relationships. Worry and concern about her is understandable. Her situation can improve if she is willing to take more responsibility for herself, read helpful books, talk with others, etc.

7-15 Points → **High.** This person's actions have serious negative effects upon his life and the lives of those around him. This is likely to show up in several areas of his life. He can make changes if he is willing to get significant support from organized groups or mental health professionals.

16-26 Points → **Very High.** A loved one functioning in this range has very serious problems. These problems undoubtedly show up not only with close family members and friends but also at work, school, and other areas of their daily life. In order to improve, this person probably needs considerable long-term professional intervention.

The next section, and the rest of *It's So Hard to Love You*, will help you figure out what to do with the score you've just arrived at for your troubled friend or relative. No matter what the score is, we have tools and suggestions that will help you decide what you want to do.

Evaluating Harmfulness

At this point, let's look at another way you can evaluate how harmful your difficult loved one's actions are. This evaluation is based on four factors: 1) the frequency of the problem behaviors, 2) their severity, 3) feedback from others, and 4) your own intuition. Let's look at the four factors.

FREQUENCY

A good way to rate a person's behavior is to notice how often negative incidents come up. Actions that might be acceptable on rare occasions become unacceptable if they happen repeatedly. In fact, repetition of mistakes is a hallmark of difficult people. They seem to make the same poor decisions over and over.

For example, very occasionally shouting in anger is not necessarily okay, but it may be understandable. Shouting once a month, once a week, or once a day is another thing entirely. Being fired from a job once or twice in a lifetime is something that many people might experience. Getting fired from one job after another is a sign that someone has a real problem—and it's not the employer! Drinking too much on very rare occasions may be one thing. Drinking too much once a day, once a week, or once a month is unhealthy.

SEVERITY

The severity or extent of incidents is vitally important. We are all guilty of being insensitive or inconsiderate at times, but big hurts are different. They stay in the memory and do far more harm.

For example, telling a child you'll see her at a certain time and then showing up a few minutes late is probably forgotten when you do show up and apologize. Promising to be there but not showing up at all leaves a wound. Assertively raising your voice in frustration may be healthy on occasion. Screaming, swearing, and name-calling is not. Borrowing five dollars and forgetting to pay it back might not be a problem. However, borrowing five hundred dollars and never giving it back is a big problem—as you will relearn each time you lend that person money.

FEEDBACK FROM OTHERS

If you haven't already done so, talk about your TLO to a close friend, family member, spiritual leader, counselor, or other trusted person. Describe what your TLO has been doing and how you've been reacting. You're likely to receive valuable insights. Just the process of telling your story is often helpful. You might uncover truths you hadn't seen.

The opinions of trusted friends and family can help you separate healthy actions from unhealthy ones. If people you trust tell you they see a problem, listen carefully, even if it is hard and uncomfortable. Ask directly for their opinions. They might have strong views but feel reluctant to give you "unsolicited advice." You, of course, determine whether to follow their advice, but learning what others think can teach you a lot about yourself and your situation.

You might find it embarrassing to confide in others. You might fear their judgment or criticism. The way to avoid harsh reactions is to pick your listener carefully. Go to someone who has treated you well in the past and has a positive approach to life. Talk to someone who will give you her undivided attention.

YOUR OWN INTUITION

Pay attention to your gut reactions. Trust your own internal voice, or intuition, because it generally has something helpful to offer.

What does intuition feel like? How do you know when to follow it and when not to? The experience we're talking about is usually a calm sort of feeling somewhere inside you. It can feel like a slight preference for one choice over another or a definite feeling of yes or no. It might just pop into your head or slide in out of the blue. Sometimes, intuition shows up in a series of "coincidences" that you notice very clearly. Although gut feelings and internal voices are hard to define, the more you tune in to yours, the better you'll get at hearing them. And as you do so, you will, like many people, learn to trust the accuracy of your inner voice. Keep practicing. It will get easier.

The exercise below will help you assess how harmful your TLO's actions are in light of the four factors listed above. As you're working on this (or any) exercise, other reactions may come up within you that aren't directly related to the table you're filling in or the journal entry you're writing. For example, it would not be unusual for you to feel tension in your back or jaw, find it hard to catch your breath, feel sad, and/or have all sorts of thoughts intruding on the work you're trying to do here. These are normal reactions to stress. Some good ways to deal with these reactions are to:

- Tell yourself you'll deal with each "intrusive" thought and feeling later (and be sure to do so).

- Stop for just a moment and stretch, get a drink of water, ask for a hug, etc.

■ Briefly jot down your intrusive thoughts somewhere else and get back to them later.

The point is that while it's completely normal for all kinds of other feelings and thoughts (such as shopping lists or people you have to call tonight) to jump in at the "wrong" time, it's best not to give them much attention when you're working on something else. Set those intruding thoughts aside for the time being and get back to the task at hand.

As always, if you have more than one TLO, do this exercise for each one separately. Use your journal to evaluate more behaviors or to record other thoughts and feelings that arise as you do this whole exercise. An example has been done for you throughout the exercise.

Evaluating Your TLO's Behavior

First of all, list what you consider to be the three most troublesome of your TLO's actions or ways of speaking. Be quite specific, so it's easier to evaluate each behavior. For example, rather than say, "She ignores me and everybody else and throws stuff around all the time," separate those behaviors and deal with each one on its own. Write, "She ignores me" and "She breaks her own and other people's stuff."

1. _____

2. _____

3. _____

Now, work with these three behaviors you've chosen in the rest of this exercise.

FREQUENCY

We understand that some TLOs do not have an easily recognized pattern to their actions. One person might only be depressed during the winter, while another has been ignoring her spouse off and on for years. Even if your TLO doesn't have a regular pattern, you can use the table below to describe the frequency of her actions. Briefly list each troublesome action in column 1. Then for each of the three behaviors you list, check one box that best describes how frequently your TLO does that behavior.

Your TLO's 3 actions	A few times a year	A few times a month	A few times a week	A few times a day
Ex.: She ignores me.		✓		
1.				
2.				
3.				

SEVERITY

Deciding the severity of something is a personal judgment that will differ from person to person. Still, it's a good idea for you to decide for yourself how severe you think your TLO's actions are. Ask yourself questions to "measure" severity, such as: "Does she state her opinion, or does she yell?" "Does he occasionally gamble some of his spending money or regularly gamble his rent money?" "Does he chat with people on the Internet or pick up strangers in bars?" For each of the three behaviors you've listed, check the column you feel best describes the severity of that action or mood. Then for each one, also write why you have chosen that level of severity.

Your TLO's 3 Actions	Mild	Moderate	Severe
Ex.: She ignores me.		✓	
I checked "moderate" because sometimes Julia ignores us for two or three days, but never longer than that, like Ben's aunt does. She won't talk to anybody for weeks at a time. I hate when Julia does ignore us, but I can see it could be much worse. Still, I wish she did it less or not at all!			
1.			
2.			
3.			

FEEDBACK FROM OTHERS

In terms of the three problematic actions you've been working with, write in your journal what people have said about each. Whether they've been saying something for a while now, or you ask them specifically for this exercise, write down everything they say about the three actions you're working on right now. Remember, you don't have to like or agree with their feedback. Simply listen to it and write it down.

YOUR OWN INTUITION

First, write in your journal what you have thought all along about your TLO's three actions. What has your gut been telling you? Take your time. Think back. Include any or all of your past feelings, thoughts, and gut reactions regarding the three actions.

Once you've finished considering your intuitive feelings about the three actions, review this whole section, Evaluating Harmfulness, including your answers in the tables above and your writings in your journal. After you've done that, write whatever comes to mind about you, your TLO, and your overall opinion about how harmful his or her actions have been. As you continue working through *It's So Hard to Love You*, the work you're doing now will help you move forward.

ASSESSING YOUR FEELINGS ABOUT THE RELATIONSHIP

Now is a good time to pull together the thoughts, ideas, questions, and feelings you've come across so far in this chapter. In your journal, write about your TLO's behaviors and other traits you've thought about so far. Reflect on what you've learned from the exercises in this chapter. Look at your reactions to the chapter in general. To get started, answer these questions:

- How often does my troubled loved one engage in frustrating or harmful behaviors?

- Which of his behaviors are the most harmful? Whom do they harm?

- Which behaviors cause me the most distress?

- How long has she been this way?

- Do I see my relative or friend differently since reading this chapter? If so, how?

- Do I feel differently about myself since reading this chapter? If so, how?

Remember as you journal that there are no right or wrong answers. Your journal entries are your views. They aren't what somebody else thinks, or what somebody else wants you to think (including us!).

WHERE DO YOU GO FROM HERE?

By starting to see your troubling relative or friend more clearly, you've already begun to deal more effectively with your situation. As you move through this book, you'll continue to learn ideas and techniques that will bring insights about yourself and your loved one. You'll learn to:

- Manage the cascade of emotions that overwhelm you

- Communicate more clearly

- Take better care of yourself

- Set boundaries, negotiate interactions, and create contracts

- Make effective and loving decisions

YOU CONTROL YOUR LIFE

Although the person you care about may not change, you can change. You do not have to be a victim or a caretaker to anyone, no matter how much you love him or her. You don't have to be ruled by his excesses, limitations, aggression, or apathy. You can enjoy a loving life with greater peace, wholeness, and emotional intimacy than you ever imagined. And you already have all the resources you need within you right now. We'll help you find and use those resources in the coming chapters. Remember, you control your life.

2

What's Going On with Me?

Like many people with difficult relatives, Karen had done everything she could to understand and help her husband. Over the years, Martin had become increasingly withdrawn and lethargic. No matter what she did, Karen felt like they were growing further and further apart. She was determined to stay with Martin, but his aloofness was taking its toll on her and on their marriage. Karen hardly ever felt good anymore, and she found herself blaming Martin for hurting their home life. Actually, it seemed like there wasn't any home life anymore.

One evening, Karen drove home from work along the "scenic route," as Martin used to call it. She thought back, dwelling on their early years together, when they were happy and connected. But then the more recent memories came back—Martin pulling away from her or snapping at her for no good reason, or, worse, ignoring her completely. No conversations, no fun, practically no sex. She felt like she was begging if she asked him to go someplace with her. Karen was finding it all really hard, and she felt almost no hope that she'd ever get her husband and their happy life back.

Soon the homestretch appeared, bringing her closer to the driveway and the front door she'd begun to dread. With dismay, Karen thought, "When did I start to hate coming home?" She managed to paste on a smile just as the front door swung open, but the dead silence that greeted her told her nothing was any different than it had been last night or the many nights before. Martin was probably stuck upstairs on that damned computer again—cold and boring as ever.

She wanted to scream and cry and run back out the door, and at the same time she felt really angry. "I just can't do this anymore! There has to be a better way." Karen turned around right then and drove to her friend Sasha's house. Sasha had been telling Karen for months that she didn't have to figure this all out by herself. She had lots of choices to help herself live—not just survive—with Martin. Maybe it was time to listen.

Karen had tried every single thing she could think of to make things better for Martin and herself. She kept trying to live the life she wanted, but it wasn't working. Martin kept repeating his frustrating actions, and Karen kept running after him trying to fix things—and getting angrier. She felt totally confused and sick at heart.

Certainly, Martin's withdrawal from her had affected their marriage. But the puzzling and uncomfortable truth is that Karen's ongoing efforts to fix things had also affected their marriage. At first, she thought that if she just loved him and was patient, Martin would "snap out of it." When he didn't, she tried many ways to help him do that. She suggested counseling, training for a new career, new hobbies, and old hobbies. She took on more of the home responsibilities and accepted extra hours at work. Her own social life shrank because she was too tired and preoccupied to go out with her friends.

Over time, Karen felt more and more discouraged and resentful, but she felt guilty about that, so she pushed those feelings away and told herself "Be patient. Hold on. Just love him, and he'll go back to the way he used to be."

But none of those things worked because Karen was directing all that energy for change at the wrong person. Karen's friend, Sasha, helped her begin to see that she could not change Martin—look how hard she'd tried, yet it hadn't worked. Sasha pointed Karen in a more effective direction by helping her realize she could only change herself. Martin was Martin's business. Karen was Karen's business.

This chapter is devoted to helping you look at and understand what's going on with you in your relationship with your TLO. As you work through the chapter, give yourself breaks when you need them; you're digging into difficult territory.

A NEW DIRECTION

When you care about someone, it's natural to want to help him. It's also natural to want to avoid struggle and hurt. But what often happens in difficult relationships is that people have trouble seeing what's really going on, what's underneath the surface. They can see what others do and say, but they don't understand where the actions and words come from. And they often feel equally confused by their own words and actions, not understanding how things got the way they are.

If you feel like that, then you might find your thoughts and feelings sometimes swirling around inside, whipping up a storm that threatens to overwhelm you. At other times, you might feel "dead" inside, too numb or too sick and tired of the whole thing to care. You might have thoughts you feel terrible about, because you're a good person, and you do love this troublesome person. Maybe you say and do things you regret. Maybe you do nothing at all.

So discouraging. So confusing!

If, like Karen, you've tried every single thing you can think of to help your TLO, you might feel heartsick and angry, too. Or maybe you still think you can help him if you just do more of this or less of that. The reality is that if your friend or relative is not ready to change his ways, there's absolutely nothing you can do to make him be ready. But that is not the end of your story—it's the beginning.

As Sasha told Karen, the solutions to your difficulties do not lie in the other person, or in what he does, or in what you do to fix him. The solutions are inside you. Your efforts to help your loved one may have been understandable and even heroic. But if they haven't managed to improve his life (and your own), then this might be a good time to try something different.

The "something different" we're talking about is an approach to life called "letting go with love." This approach does not mean you have to let go of the person or get her out of your life (although you might end up deciding to do that). It doesn't mean you tell yourself his problematic actions don't matter. What letting go with love does mean is this:

1. You can accept difficult people without accepting their harmful behavior.

2. Taking care of yourself is a loving thing to do that also benefits others.

In this chapter, you'll begin to examine how you've already tried to fix your situation or your TLO; how the situation got to be the way it is; and how you think and feel about it all. It's very much like sorting out a junk drawer. Before you can make it better, you have to deal with what's already there.

You will learn you cannot make your TLO be what you wish she would be, but you can be who *you* want to be. There's even a bonus—being yourself turns out to be the most positive contribution you can make to any relationship.

YOUR ACTIONS—WHAT HAVE YOU ALREADY TRIED?

In order to understand how things got to be the way they are, begin by "cataloguing" your efforts to fix your TLO. The following exercise will help you recognize and acknowledge what you do and say in this challenging relationship. The list contains a number of common reactions to other people's crazy-making behavior. With your problem person in mind, check all the actions you have done or threatened to do in the last year. If you think of other actions that aren't on the list, write them in your journal. By assessing your actions on paper, you can get a little distance from them—and that is an important part of untangling a messy situation.

Be as honest with yourself as you can be. This can be uncomfortable, but it's kind of like taking a sliver out of your finger. It hurts a bit, but afterwards it feels much better.

Reviewing Your Actions

Check the actions you do in your troubled relationship.	✓
Give in, keep out of her way, or speak in soothing tones to avoid rocking the boat.	
Eat or sleep too much or too little.	

Give him rides, take care of his kids, etc., when he runs into problems.	
Apologize for getting angry or for crying.	
Beg, cry, yell, or scream.	
Lend or give her money, food, or other things.	
Point out how embarrassing her behavior is to herself and others.	
Appeal to her "better" self—the responsible parent, the good daughter, the reliable employee, the wage earner.	
Smile or laugh to cover your true feelings.	
Do things to please him in the hope he'll appreciate you and treat you better.	
Not look at him or not speak to him.	
Act worse than he does, hoping he'll get the message.	
Keep busy to avoid your feelings.	
Tell yourself or others it's not so bad.	
Lie or make excuses to cover up for her behavior.	
Take the blame for things you didn't do, to protect someone else.	
Avoid people and activities you enjoy.	
Make allowances because of challenges she faces or has faced.	
Keep secrets.	
Make decisions for him or tell him what to do.	
Threaten to leave.	
Work twice as hard to make up for what he doesn't do.	

Was it hard to see yourself in this list? Maybe it was a relief. Were you surprised by any of the statements you checked? Did you discover anything new about yourself? Write your thoughts in your journal.

Exploring your own actions can help you understand yourself better, as Taneesha learned in the following situation.

I always had an excuse for my boyfriend, or I'd find one. I thought everything was my fault. Maybe I dressed too tight. Maybe I looked at somebody and should've kept my head down. He was allowed to go out, but I wasn't. If I did, I'd get hurt or yelled at and screamed at. Then he'd start calling me at 4 A.M. . . . starting when the bar closed and sometimes till 6 A.M. I was exhausted from talking on the phone and staying up all night. He'd be mad at me because he went out all night and got drunk and was so tired from the nightlife.

It was starting to make sense to me at the end. I learned in counseling and in the women's center that nothing I did would change him. And I learned I shouldn't be treated that way.

As you continue through *It's So Hard to Love You*, you'll learn how to change your actions that don't help you. At the moment, though, it will be helpful to explore your thoughts and feelings, because they drive your actions. Paying attention to what you think and feel will help you understand why you do what you do and how you got where you are.

YOUR THOUGHTS—WHAT'S GOING ON IN YOUR HEAD?

You've begun to sort out your actions in this relationship, but actions don't occur in a vacuum. They are an outward expression of something deeper—your thoughts and feelings. It's important to sort through these, too, just as you've done with your actions. Your thoughts are powerful. You can learn to take charge of your life by learning to recognize which thoughts help you and which ones don't.

To become more conscious of your thoughts, do the following exercise. Read the list of thoughts commonly experienced by others who care about troublesome people. Check the ones you have thought regarding your TLO. Take your time. This isn't a competition, but if it were, it would be won by going slowly and carefully.

Reviewing Your Thoughts

I think ...	✓
1. Look at how she's suffered already.	
2. He refuses to listen when I remind him about his responsibilities.	
3. She needs my guidance.	
4. They/I shouldn't be so hard on him. He can't help it.	
5. I'll just do this for him once more, to help him get back on his feet.	
6. It's nobody else's business what goes on.	
7. Nobody cares what's happening to me.	
8. I feel so alone.	
9. Nobody sees how bad it is.	
10. If he cared about me, he wouldn't act that way.	
11. What's wrong with me?	
12. If I were a better parent (spouse, sister, etc.), he wouldn't do those things.	
13. Why would I think I could do anything right? I never have yet.	
14. It's my fault, because I'm so stupid (ugly, useless, etc.).	
15. Somebody else will be mad at me if I don't hang in there with her.	
16. I'm going to live my own life as best I can.	
17. It'd be so great if she would talk to a counselor or somebody.	
18. Maybe the minister will have some suggestions for me.	
19. She'd be much happier if she quit living that way. I hope she figures it out soon.	
20. He does so many dumb things; I'm glad he doesn't live with us anymore.	

Each group of statements above represents an underlying approach people often take to problematic people. Read the explanations below to better understand what your thoughts tell you about yourself in relation to your TLO.

Statements 1-5 indicate you might believe it's your job to take care of your loved one and try to fix him or his problems. One term for this way of thinking is "enmeshment." An enmeshed approach prevents the other person from making his own choices and mistakes. Enmeshed people often end up feeling stuck and frustrated, and maybe even sick, when they try to force solutions. Learning to let go with love will help you and your troubled loved one carry your own loads.

Statements 6-10 indicate you might feel isolated or lonely because of your situation. By reaching out for help, you will gain much-needed support and relief. Your struggles can diminish when you share them with a trusted listener.

Statements 11-15 indicate that you might think you are defective. This way of thinking is very draining, and it is simply not true. Have you ever heard the saying "God don't make no junk"? Well, that's true for you, just as much as it's true for anybody else. Besides, not being able to fix the other person is not a defect—it's a basic fact of life. No one can do that—except that person.

Statements 16-20 can indicate you're aware there's a problem, but you realize that neither you nor your TLO is defective. The situation might be maddening and discouraging, but you have a good idea that actions do not indicate the worth of a person. You're able to separate yourself from the troubling person's problems, at least to some extent. Such an approach is a crucial part of letting go with love.

Seeing your thought patterns more clearly will help you understand how you got to the point you have. Then you can begin changing whatever is not working for you.

YOUR EMOTIONS—WHAT'S GOING ON IN YOUR HEART?

Difficult events stir emotions. This is natural; it's the way people are. You could think of emotions as a signal to notice and do something about what's happening.

Emotions provide the fuel for your actions and thoughts, and they can show up in various ways. Sometimes feelings practically explode, sparking thoughts and actions that don't add anything positive to a situation. At other times, they seem to roll in like fog—so invisible you only notice them when tears start rolling down your cheeks or your fists clench so tight your knuckles hurt.

It can be hard to recognize what you feel when so much is going on in your life. And what about when you face the same situations over and over again, as you probably do with your TLO? Well, what often happens is that people learn not to notice, or even feel, their feelings at all. They often describe this internal climate as "nothing," "dead," "numb," or "cold." This "nonfeeling" feeling is a common internal response to emotional overload.

However, even if you've learned to shut down or ignore your anger, sadness, disappointment, and other hard feelings, they still happen inside you. When feelings don't get noticed or expressed, they can go "underground" and result in physical illness or other problems. Therefore, it's important to get to know your feelings. They are not the enemy; their job is to help you see and experience whatever is happening so you can make clearer decisions, enjoy life, and connect to the world around you. In the quote below, George tells how he got started exploring his feelings.

> *I was trying to figure out how to live with my wife without losing my mind. One of my buddies kept telling me to get some help, so I finally decided to give it a try. I started going to a support group. At first it felt weird, but kind of good, too. These people knew what I was talking about! Once I got comfortable, I unloaded my problems to them, and they listened. It felt pretty good to finally have somebody to talk to about all the maddening stuff she did. Then at one meeting, I told about how my wife had "forgotten" about another appointment we had*

and how irresponsible and selfish she was. One of the members asked me, "How do you feel about what your wife did?" That caught me off guard. After a couple seconds I said I didn't know. And he said, "Well, you sure know a lot about your wife. Maybe now it's time for you to learn about yourself." That really helped me get started on my own recovery.

As George found out, it is possible to figure out what's going on inside as well as outside yourself. You can do this, too.

The table on the next page contains three columns of feeling-words. As you read each word, notice if it rings true for you. Check every emotion you feel or have felt in connection with your difficult relative or friend.

YOUR FEELINGS, THOUGHTS, AND ACTIONS—TYING THEM ALL TOGETHER

We began this section by asking you to notice your actions, then your thoughts and feelings. We dealt with actions first because they're generally easier to identify than thoughts and feelings. But now that you've done all three exercises, keep in mind that human experience actually goes in the opposite direction. When something happens, we usually feel first, and then think or act. Additional feelings, thoughts, and actions may jump in there in quick succession. Being able to notice and name what's going on with your actions, thoughts, and feelings puts you in a much better position to do something constructive with them.

The key ideas in this section have been:

- Your actions, thoughts, and feelings are natural and common to many people. Others often react the way you do with challenging loved ones.

- You have the ability to think about your feelings, thoughts, and actions in detail. Doing so prepares you to make changes that will work for you.

- You have the ability to deal with what you learn about yourself.

Assessing Your Feelings

I feel …	✓	I feel …	✓	I feel …	✓
abused		frustrated		patient	
afraid		furious		pessimistic	
alone		guilty		protective	
angry		happy		provoked	
appreciated		hateful		resentful	
blamed		helpless		responsible	
bored		hopeful		right	
bullied		hopeless		sad	
calm		hurt		safe	
confident		ignored		stupid	
confused		impatient		successful	
connected		important		suicidal	
depressed		incompetent		terrified	
disconnected		invisible		trapped	
disliked		irritated		unappreciated	
drained		lost		unhappy	
embarrassed		loving		unloved	
forgetful		misunderstood		unsafe	
frantic		nervous		unsupported	
frazzled		overwhelmed		weary	
free		overworked		worried	

Just as you did with the Reviewing Your Actions table, ask yourself some questions. Were you surprised at the feeling-words you checked? Did you learn anything new about yourself? Explore your discoveries, questions, and answers in your journal or with someone you trust.

FUZZY LOGIC, FUZZY LOVE

You've now identified and explored some of your own actions, thoughts, and feelings. That's a great step toward positive change. Now let's look in more detail at your reactions to your TLO.

Like others who care about a difficult person, you probably didn't think your life would turn out the way it has. No one plans to have children who become adult victims or manipulators. When someone marries the love of his life, he can't predict that she'll later become depressed, vindictive, or obsessive. What in the world happens to people?

Life happens to people. People make choices every minute, based on what they believe about themselves, their lives, and their relationships. Their choices are influenced by when and where they live; their parents and culture; personality and gender; experiences with success and struggle; physical characteristics; and more. All those influences, mixed with their own thoughts, beliefs, and feelings, can turn into quite a soup!

The confusion that sometimes results is what we call "fuzzy logic, fuzzy love." It can be very hard to sort your own thoughts, feelings, and preferences from those of your TLO or other people you care about. For example, how do your mother's beliefs about family responsibility jibe with your beliefs? If you really love (or fear) your mom, you might feel unsure what to do if you don't share her beliefs. And if you disagree, are you being disloyal or unloving? Maybe you're not sure which parts you agree with and which you don't. And if she criticizes you every time she calls you, because she isn't happy with how you're living your life, it can be hard to know how to think or feel about it yourself. Numerous factors tumble and smash together, creating confusion and exhaustion. There is rarely a clear, black and white answer for such predicaments, but you can definitely find greater clarity.

One remedy for fuzzy logic and fuzzy love is to separate family history, personal experiences, feelings, thoughts, and actions into workable "pieces and piles." (Remember the junk drawer?) Start by examining the factors that affect the relationship with your TLO.

The ten factors that follow contribute to and result from the jumble of attitudes, feelings, and thoughts many people have about themselves and their TLOs. Examining each factor will help you sort through your own feelings and thoughts. This sorting will, in turn, help you gain insight into what makes you tick so you can clear away some of the fuzziness you're experiencing. The ten factors are:

1. Love

2. Fear

3. Resentment and anger

4. Blame

5. Guilt

6. Shame

7. Compassion fatigue

8. Magical thinking

9. Obligations and duty

10. Expectations

Some of these factors may not apply to you, but they are common stumbling blocks for many people and can help explain how you got where you are today. The information below does not present absolutes, because absolutes in human relations are rare. However, by contemplating the ten factors, you can better understand yourself—a crucial part of growth and healing.

Love

Now there's a topic. It's a challenge to define love in a sentence or two, or even in a book or two. Yet you can experience it in the silence of a moment or in the soft tracing of your finger across a loved one's cheek.

Humans yearn for love, use it as a weapon, and shout it from the rooftops—and, still, love is a mystery. It is the wonderful, energizing core of human existence. But it certainly is not always easy to understand. So how, especially when you're hurting or worried, do you figure out what to do about love? Is it enough to stay around for? How does it mix with duty and commitment? How do you even know if you love someone? Can love die?

These questions need to be asked because love—and your ideas about it—coexists with everything else you feel for your relative or friend. Here is a list of statements about loving someone. Check the statements that match how you feel about your TLO.

_____ When we aren't together, I miss her and want to be with her.

_____ I enjoy our time together.

_____ I feel warmth in my heart when I think about him.

_____ His life is interesting to me.

_____ I feel responsible for her.

_____ My religious or moral beliefs tell me to do whatever I can to help, no matter what.

_____ I can count on her to help me when I need it.

_____ I feel grateful when I think about his presence in my life.

_____ I admire the way she lives her life.

_____ I love her just because we're married/related/friends.

_____ We can usually sort things out honestly after an argument.

_____ I'm free to live my life the way I want, and so is he.

_____ I respect her.

_____ I'm determined to show her how much I love her.

_____ He delights me most of the time.

_____ I value our relationship because of our shared history.

Have you met with any surprises? In your journal, write anything you've noticed about your love for your trouble loved one.

Fear

Fear is at the root of every human struggle. It is experienced in many guises and to varying degrees. Fear can take hold of your mind and twist your insides into knots. Its power over people is undeniable—but it does not have to be that way. Fear can be faced and managed, even overcome. To do that, one must take the first step—understanding. Some common fears that hold people in difficult situations are:

- **Fear of being alone:** nobody else would want me. I wouldn't be able to stand the loneliness.

- **Fear of failing:** I've already screwed up so many times. What if I make another mistake?

- **Fear of being judged:** what will they say if I tell him no? Aren't I a bad person if I don't help her?

- **Fear of financial problems:** I can't make it on my small paycheck. I don't want to move to a smaller place.

- **Fear of conflict:** I can't do that; he might get upset. I hope she's in a good mood today.

- **Fear of fear:** I don't want to feel this way. It's too scary.

If you can relate to any of these fears, you know how hard and fast they can grab you. Even reading about fear might feel scary. That's natural. Take a few deep breaths to get some oxygen to your brain and to calm your heart. Remind yourself that fear is a feeling; it does not have to stop you from acting. Throughout this book you will learn to gain more control over your feelings—even the fear of fear.

Resentment and Anger

Most people are familiar with anger, and some recognize resentment, anger's parent. Resentment is the parent because it often comes first and provides a breeding ground for anger. Resentment can be hard to notice. It's the squinty-eyed little monster grumbling away in the background, building up strength until it's ready to give birth to anger.

The voice of resentment says, "How could she do that to me?" or "I shouldn't have to put up with this." Resentment justifies itself and greedily holds on to every offense it believes has occurred.

Resentment and anger are not pretty parts of anyone's makeup, but they seem to be a common response to harm and perceived harm. The fact that they're common, however, doesn't mean you have to indulge and nurture them. Use them as all emotions can be used—to notice what's going on around and within you. Harness their energy to make changes in your life—without damaging yourself or anyone else. Learn to let go of resentment and anger before they poison you and those around you.

Blame

Resentment has another offspring, and it is called blame. This "child" can look just as unpleasant as its parent—a tight-lipped creature with a pointing finger, always ready to assign fault. Blame believes that all problems and solutions come from "out there." It wants somebody else to be responsible for problems, because taking responsibility for oneself isn't always easy. The trouble with harboring blame is that it keeps the blamer stuck. It keeps you from realizing that solutions are within your reach. As soon as that finger stops pointing, it can again become a useful member of your hand—a hand that can do something positive.

Guilt

This is another complex emotion. Guilt is the belief that you've done something wrong. Let's say Suzanne has told Maria she'll go to Maria's graduation ceremony on Saturday. Late Friday afternoon, Suzanne gets a chance to go on an optional training course she's been dreaming about. She calls Maria from work and tells her she "has to go for work." Her friend is very disappointed, but she understands, believing that Suzanne's boss is making her go. After a while, Suzanne feels terrible. She's responsible for this lie and is, therefore, guilty. She has a healthy awareness of having done wrong.

If not faced squarely, guilt eats away at you and becomes a burden. At some point, it's important to forgive yourself and move on. Okay, you made a mistake. Own up to it, do what you can to fix it, and get on with your life. Learn not to make that mistake again. Let go of the guilt.

Suzanne could have carried her guilt around for a long time, but she didn't. She realized her lie might have done great harm to her relationship with Maria, so she took her courage in hand and told Maria what she'd done. She resolved never to do such a thing again. What's more, once she'd dealt with the lie, Suzanne refused to listen to her guilty thoughts. She learned from that mistake and got on with her life by letting go of the guilt.

Sometimes a person will try to make someone else feel guilty. They usually do this to hide from their own responsibilities. But no one can make you feel anything. Look closely at the situation and decide for yourself if you've done something you consider to be wrong. If so, deal with it. If not, don't take on someone else's idea of what you should or should not do.

Shame

Shame is a toxic, negative emotion. Shame is often confused with guilt, and it can be thought of in two ways—both of which drain away your vitality.

The first form of shame is the clinging belief that you have little or no value because of something you've done. This type of shame usually results from unresolved guilty feelings (for something you actually did do that you regret). Suzanne, from the example above, might have felt shame if she had not faced up to her lie or had continued to blame herself for lying to Maria.

Just as other people might stop trusting Suzanne, she might start to believe she didn't deserve to be trusted. Eventually, she would learn not to trust herself and would believe the worst about herself. Her shame over her mistake could become toxic and very hard to get rid of. She'd be fairly likely to make more poor choices and unconsciously seek out people who would reinforce her shameful belief about herself. And she'd probably find them.

The second form of shame is the belief that you *are* something wrong—that you are flawed and horrible. This type of shame often results when you've been victimized and degraded in some way. For example, people who have been sexually assaulted tend to take on this type of shame because they believe they should have been able to stop the assault but were too stupid, weak, cowardly, or useless to do so. Because sexual assault and other forms of degradation are still widely misunderstood, many individuals reinforce these beliefs. Such beliefs are not correct, and they damage many people's trust in themselves.

If you feel shame, we encourage you to talk about it with a supportive person. You can heal and free yourself from shame, even if the shame you feel ties you to a difficult person. Many, many people have done so. Then you can make a clearer decision about your connection to your TLO.

Compassion Fatigue

Compassion is a wonderful human emotion. It's what you feel when you see someone struggling or suffering and you have a desire to help. Compassion is the author of many good works. Compassion fatigue, on the other hand, is a state of tired indifference that results from repeated exposure to disappointment or frustration.

For instance, if your sister, April, calls to tell you she's been fired, you might feel pity, surprise, concern, etc. You might respond with offers of help and support. These are natural compassionate responses.

Now imagine you've just found out from a friend that April's been fired again—her fifth time. (She doesn't call to tell you anymore.) You still experience a range of feelings and thoughts, but they're probably quite different than they were the first time she was fired. Because you've been down this road several times before, you're getting pretty tired of it. You might still be worried about her, but you also feel frustrated and confused about how she can keep letting this happen. You probably don't want to hear any more of her "stupid boss and lousy job" excuses.

That's what compassion fatigue is like. It accounts for the long sighs and deep weariness that result from ongoing, repeated disappointment and frustration. After a while, you find it hard to care what kind of trouble your TLO gets into.

Magical Thinking

Magical thinking is another aspect of fuzzy logic, fuzzy love. Magical thinking is an approach to life that often starts in childhood and is based on the belief that either good luck or someone bigger, smarter, stronger, or braver will help you or fix something in your life. "Maybe I'll win the lottery. Then my money worries will be over." "Henry will take care of that. I'm no good at such things."

Magical thinking is expressed in several childhood story ideals:

- Follow the yellow brick road.

- ... and they lived happily ever after.

- Once upon a time ...

The trouble with such sentiments is not that people enjoyed and believed in them as children or that they believe in them as adults. The problem is that many adults rely solely on the vague hope that some person or event will come along and fix whatever is not going well. Such reliance on mystical wishes prevents many adults from recognizing their own ability and power to act.

If you call magical thinking by another name—hope—you can retain some of the magic and sparkle that is childhood's gift, while still being realistic about yourself and your life. You can draw strength from hope as you do what needs to be done and accept your circumstances for what they are—not what you wish they'd be.

Magical Thinking Inventory

Pick one of the three examples of magical thinking above that you put some stock in. Reflect on that idea and write about how it has shaped your adult life. Think about whether your belief is helpful or not helpful in your dealings with your TLO.

_____

_____

_____

_____

Obligations and Duty

Ideas about duty and obligation are created by the society, time, and culture in which you live. They perform important functions in any society by keeping life predictable and helping people define their roles. Duties and rules generally support order rather than chaos.

However, the fact that duty is usually determined by something outside yourself can also be a problem. Confusion reigns when you don't understand the duties you feel obliged to carry out, or why, or who says so. For our purposes here, it doesn't matter so much where your feelings of obligation come from (though digging into that can be interesting and enlightening). It matters more right now that you begin to recognize what ideas about obligation and duty you believe in. Then you can decide which ones are working for you and which aren't.

To learn more about this, answer the following questions in your journal. Think especially about yourself and your TLO as you do so.

- What do I do out of a sense of obligation?

- What feelings rose up as I thought about that question?

- Which of my obligations feel good to me?

- Which obligations don't feel so good?

Expectations

People have a variety of ideas about expectations. Some people think you should expect others, especially family, to do certain things in certain ways. Others say that if you never expect anything, you'll never be disappointed. What does it mean to have an expectation? When are expectations all right, and when aren't they? There are no absolutes, but here are some ideas to consider when thinking about expectations:

- An expectation is not the same as a request. With a request, there is no wrong response. The other person is free to be honest. With an expectation, on the other hand, a certain response is required, and that greatly decreases the chances for honesty.

- Expectations between adults greatly narrow the possibility of freedom, acceptance, and love—for both parties.

- Acceptance is the opposite of expectation.

- It has been said that expectations are premeditated resentments.

- When you strongly feel it is reasonable to expect something of another adult, make your expectation clear. State what you would like and why. Be willing to accept a "no" answer, without punishing the other person.

- Don't expect or try to change a trait you don't like in someone else. No one can change anyone else. You might succeed in making life so unpleasant that the disagreeable trait goes "underground," but that isn't real change.

- Generally speaking, the less you expect others to meet your requirements, the less disappointed and frustrated you'll be.

When are expectations reasonable? When you're expecting a baby. When you expect a chair to hold your weight. When someone says they'll do something. When all parties clearly agree to an idea, approach, or plan of action.

Expectations

In your journal, respond to these statements and questions.

- List two or three expectations you have of your troublesome relative or friend.

- How do these expectations usually work out?

- Why do you think they do or don't work out?

- When they do work out, how do you feel?

- When they don't work out, how do you feel?

- How do you feel when someone expects you to do or be something they have in mind for you?

Logic and Love—No Longer Quite So Fuzzy?

In this section you've considered ten factors that affect you and your relationship with a difficult person. We hope your work has enabled you to clarify some aspects of that relationship. Keep in mind that, as a rule, awareness and change happen slowly. And that is just fine, because most people need time to get used to new ideas and feelings.

NOW THAT I'VE SORTED THE JUNK DRAWER, WHAT DO I DO WITH ALL THE STUFF I FOUND?

If you had actually cleaned out a junk drawer, what would you be looking at right now? You'd have little piles of dusty screws and nails; three old scissors; five half-gone matchbooks; etc. Looking at all that stuff, you might just want to scoop it all into the trash. But you've gone to all the bother of sorting it, so you might as well see what's worth keeping and put it someplace useful.

New Awareness Inventory

The same goes for all the thoughts, feelings, and actions you've sorted through in this chapter. Here's your chance to assess the "stuff" you've found so far. On the lines below, list a few of the things you've learned or realized in this chapter. Then in your journal, write about the impact your new awareness can have on you and on your relationship with your TLO.

_____

_____

_____

_____

You can learn to see the patterns that have shaped you. It doesn't matter whether you're twenty or ninety when you begin to see those patterns and influences. Awareness brings change, and you can choose to know and see in new ways. Personal growth is about turning on some emotional "lights" and brightening your outlook. Ask yourself, "What is *my* best?" rather than "What is *the* best?"

In coming chapters, you will learn more about yourself and your difficult loved one. You'll acquire more ideas and useful tools and learn how to apply them. The next chapter will give you a chance to learn and think about your TLO in new ways.

3

Understanding Your Troublesome Loved One

Estelle has a troubling loved one, her daughter, Melissa, who has been living with one man after another since she was seventeen years old. She has two young sons Estelle worries about constantly. Estelle has, sadly, become used to her daughter asking for money or a temporary place to stay, but now there's been a new development. Estelle noticed bruises on Melissa's arms the last time Melissa came over.

"Melissa, you've got marks on your arm. He did that to you, didn't he?!" Estelle exclaimed. "You've got to get away from him. You're twenty-five years old. You have to know better. He pushed you down this summer, too. When are you going to realize you can't let him treat you like that?"

"He didn't mean it, Mom. He was just upset. The kids were getting to him, and when he's not working he gets upset. He's just frustrated."

"But Melissa, he yells at you all the time, and the boys are afraid of him. How can you make your own children live with somebody like that?"

"I'm sorry, Mom. I know you worry about me, but we're okay. Really. I love him. He was just having a bad day. I was yelling too much myself. I've got to get that under control, and I know we'll get along better."

Estelle turned and strode into the living room. Frustrated thoughts bounced around in her head. "I don't know why I keep trying to talk to that girl. I might as well be talking to the wall."

Melissa watched her mother leave. Deep down, she feared her mother was right. She knew her boyfriend had a temper and could be mean and demanding with her kids. But she just couldn't make him move out. She didn't have a good job, and she had no money. He'd made her give up her friends, so now she felt like she had nobody else.

Certainly Melissa is a troubled person. She can't seem to figure out why all these bad things keep happening to her. No matter how hard she tries, she always seems to make bad choices.

TROUBLESOME LOVED ONES SHARE SIMILAR TRAITS

Although the details of Melissa's life may be quite different from those of your troubled friend or relative, there's a good chance they have some things in common. Regardless of differences in race, age, gender, income, IQ, physical appearance and ability, or anything else, troubled people are more alike than different.

In this chapter, you'll have a chance to look at the difficulties and struggles many troubling people face. As worrisome and frustrating as they can be to you, you'll be able to deal more effectively with them, and feel better yourself, if you understand some of what makes them tick. Read about the traits that many TLOs share.

Hidden Emotions

Difficult people often struggle with powerful emotions they fear will overtake them. Not knowing what else to do, they minimize or bury their feelings. They might appear to be happy, or they might use anger to cover their sadness or fear. It can be hard to talk with them about feelings, because they might not know they're hiding deeper feelings.

Low Self-Esteem

Self-esteem is a measure of a person's belief in his own worth. Many troubled people have low self-esteem. At the deepest level, they don't believe they are valuable and worthwhile. Some difficult people make their feelings of inadequacy obvious. They speak quietly, make little eye contact, and rarely voice an opinion or try new things. Others cover their feelings of inadequacy by acting superior or pushy.

Regardless of how they present themselves to others, people with low self-esteem can have great difficulty admitting mistakes or talking about shortcomings. Talking about problems is too painful because they've usually tried to change many times without success. If you've tried to talk to your difficult loved one and gotten nowhere, you know how frustrating this can be. He may retreat, change the subject, or attack. And now think of this: the frustration you feel is probably much less than his.

Poor Decisions

Difficult loved ones often make poor decisions. They misjudge situations or other people's abilities or intentions and often overestimate or underestimate their own.

A vicious cycle can begin, in which their poor decisions bring their self-confidence even lower. Then, feeling more insecure, they become less likely to ask for help or input from others. Without feedback, they continue to make the same poor decisions. They stop trusting people, including themselves. Finally, because they can't accurately see what's going on, they blame others for their own poor decisions or stop making any decisions at all.

Repeated Mistakes

A key characteristic of problematic adults is that they often repeat their mistakes over and over. They don't seem to learn from the past. Whether it's dating unhealthy partners, misspending money, losing their temper, quitting jobs, using other people, or a thousand other things, difficult loved ones don't seem to learn from their own mistakes.

TLOs deal with their repeated mistakes in a variety of ways. Some feel terrible and continually beat themselves up. Others feel badly but won't talk about it to anyone. Some deny their mistakes and refuse to accept responsibility for them.

Regardless of how they react, making the same mistakes again and again is a terrible trap for them. What are they to say after they've repeated their harmful behavior yet again? How do they make up for the harm they've done? How do they deal with your disappointment, anger, or withdrawal? How do they face themselves, or you, after they've already repeatedly apologized or promised to do better?

If you recognize your loved one's dilemma, you can better understand what she's going through, and why she does what she does.

Val is a TLO who struggled with poor self-esteem that led to unsuccessful and harmful relationships. Her stress, confusion, and shame piled up. Even though she knew her self-injuring behavior was not a "good" choice, she had a hard time stopping.

> *I had been working on healing from many years of sexual abuse. My marriage had ended, so I was a single parent with three young children. I liked my job, but it was very stressful. Somehow in the middle of all that mess, I found myself trapped in a dangerous relationship that I didn't know how to escape from. I felt responsible for all the problems in my life, whether I had caused them or not. I was ashamed of myself for being so stuck. There didn't seem to be anybody I could turn to. One day, I was sitting there feeling completely lost and overwhelmed, and I just had the thought to press my cigarette onto my arm. So I did. The pain felt satisfying. I knew at some level this wasn't a good direction to go in, but the pain on my arm overpowered the pain inside me. It gave me some relief. I burned myself several more times after that. I just didn't know what to do or how to stop.*

Temporary Changes

Troubling loved ones often make only temporary change when permanent change is needed. Although they sincerely intend to mend their ways, they seldom do. Follow-through is very difficult for them. What happens is that the strength of their commitment to change wears off. More immediate and powerful emotions take over. They forget their former promises—usually not out of malice, but out of poor self-control. Their feelings take the lead, and they repeat behavior they fully intended to avoid.

The important thing for you to realize is that their negative behavior will probably occur over and over. Don't be surprised when promised changes turn out to be short-lived. Remind yourself of this as often as you need to. Doing so will not change your loved one's behavior, but adjusting your expectations to something more realistic will lessen your own stress. And sometimes, that's all you can do.

Lack of Contentment

Contentment is a state of feeling at peace with oneself. But contentment comes from within, and that level of peace is typically not something difficult loved ones experience very often. Carlos talks about this.

> *I'm always angry. I grew up angry. I felt lonely growing up, and I didn't feel good about myself. My parents did just about nothing with me. I had only responsibilities. I saw other kids have friends, and I didn't. I cleaned out the garage while they played games. I had to save money because I was going to get thrown out of the house at eighteen. I had to work. I couldn't have fun. If I did anything wrong, I got yelled at. At age ten I'd get my ass spanked for wetting the bed every night. I remember names my father would call me like "idiot" and "bony arms." He'd say I was acting like a girl. He'd always say, "You can't do this," and "You'll do it wrong." Anger is my first reaction. I always felt like I was fighting back. Everybody else's life seems normal, and mine is different. I get bitter, and I get angry.*

Carlos has the potential to be contented, but he has a number of emotional obstacles to overcome first.

Limited Wisdom

Wisdom is the ability to understand the world and the people in it. Wisdom includes common sense and the ability to act on it. Making good decisions and taking responsibility for one's own actions are also hallmarks of the wise.

People often grow in wisdom as they age, although you may also have heard the phrase "wise beyond his years" to describe a younger person with those characteristics. In either case, wisdom is not easily obtained. It is in particularly short supply with troubled adults of all ages. Problematic loved ones are seldom thought of as wise by people who know them well.

The Wisdom Ladder

Wisdom builds on past experiences. One way to think of wisdom is to visualize it as a ladder extending high above the ground. The foot of the ladder represents a total lack of wisdom. Each rung higher represents slightly more wisdom, going up to the top rung, which represents complete knowledge and wisdom. All of us are perched somewhere on that ladder and typically move higher up as we age and mature. Here's some more information about the wisdom ladder.

Higher does not mean better. An important caution is in order here. Being higher or lower on the wisdom ladder is not about being better or worse than someone else. The wisdom ladder is intended as a way of thinking about the differing amounts of wisdom people have, not as a judgment of their worth.

Wisdom levels change. People typically move up the ladder as they grow older, although at different speeds. Unfortunately, TLOs may spend a long time on one rung that's not far off the ground.

Different levels of wisdom. People on the wisdom ladder understand the world only to their own level of wisdom. This means that people below you on the ladder can't understand or deal with situations as well as you do. The same is true for you. You can't understand what those above you can understand. No amount of wishing will give a person wisdom that is higher up the ladder than they are. Still, anyone can climb higher and achieve a clearer vision by working on their own personal growth.

Drawing a Wisdom Ladder

Try this exercise to help you better understand your difficult loved one. Draw a simple straight ladder in your journal with about fifteen or twenty rungs on it. Label it "Wisdom Ladder." The bottom rung of your ladder represents no wisdom at all, and the top rung signifies total wisdom. The middle rung represents a point where about half the adults you know would be lower and half would be higher.

Now place the name of your troubled loved one where you think he or she fits on this ladder of wisdom. Your placement represents your best guess as to his or her overall level of wisdom. If you have more than one TLO, place all their names on the ladder. Now write your name on that wisdom ladder, indicating where you think you stand.

Think now of someone you greatly respect—a positive person you think has an excellent understanding of people. This is probably someone you know, but it may be someone you simply respect from a distance. Put that person's name where you think he or she is on the ladder. You can think of this person as a role model for you.

Notice how high or low everyone is on your ladder. You could expect to see your difficult loved ones below you on the ladder and your role model at your level or—even more likely—above you. If your ladder does not look like this, take a second look at how you see the three of you and think about how much wisdom each of you has. If you want another opinion, discuss your wisdom ladder with someone you trust.

Use the lines below, and your journal, to reflect on your observations about this wisdom ladder. What characteristics of your TLO were you thinking of when you placed him where you did? Does this exercise help you understand your TLO or yourself? How?

_____

_____

_____

TLOS CAN'T SEE WHAT THEY CAN'T SEE

Some troubled people underestimate their wisdom and would put themselves lower on this ladder than they actually are. Others might put themselves higher than they actually are, thinking they know more than they do.

Your TLO might think he's wiser than he is and shout up to you from his rung on the ladder, "I see what you see! I know I'm right!" But it isn't so. This proclaiming or pleading reflects another characteristic of people who struggle on lower rungs: they can't accurately judge their level of wisdom. And they often don't know they can't judge their level of wisdom.

These folks are a little bit like a young child snitching cookies from the cookie jar. After leaving a trail of crumbs from the jar to her room, she insists she didn't do it. Any adult can see the truth; the evidence makes it obvious. But the child has not yet reached the rung on the ladder of wisdom that allows her to see what adults see.

A grown-up example of this would be your uncle's pattern of lying to cover his gambling problem. You and others see the results of his lies and mismanagement—evictions for nonpayment of rent, repeated requests to the family for loans that aren't paid back, and bill collectors at his door. Looking down from your spot on the ladder, it's all so obvious. But he has not yet learned to see his own trail of cookie crumbs.

Another example of someone on a low rung of the wisdom ladder is a negative and critical husband. You might have told him literally hundreds of times you want him to stop being so critical, but he argues with you relentlessly. He denies he's critical or blames you for it. His denials might result from self-centeredness, insecurity, upbringing, or any number of things, but the bottom line is he's not yet high enough on the ladder of wisdom (no matter how high he is on the ladder of financial or professional success) to see interpersonal relationships with the clarity you have.

Wisdom Level

To gain a bit more insight about your TLO and yourself, use the table below to describe your troublesome loved one's wisdom level, including such things as his judgment, maturity, and decision-making ability. Do this from three perspectives: what you think, what you think your TLO would say, and what you think your role model would say. For example, you might think of your TLO as clueless, he might think of himself as wise, and your role model might think of him as confused. The first line has been filled in as an example.

Your Opinion	Your TLO's Opinion	Your Role Model's Opinion
He's clueless.	I'm pretty darn smart.	He's very confused.

Take a moment to answer the following questions: What do you notice about your responses above? How are the words you think your TLO would use different from your own? How are yours different from your role model's? What do you think accounts for the differences?

_____

_____

_____

_____

Insecurity and denial are two reasons that TLOs can't see what they can't see. Take a look at the sections that follow to better understand how these reasons can play out in people's lives.

Insecurity

Often it's obvious that troubled people are insecure and feel bad about themselves. Their deepest feelings are reflected in their inability to make and stick to decisions, their trait of being influenced by others, or their inability to stand up for themselves.

But sometimes that inner weakness is not so obvious. Some loved ones appear to be powerful, determined, and decisive. But if they hurt others, they are coming from a place of emotional weakness, not strength. If they were strong enough and emotionally healthy enough to be loving, they wouldn't resort to harming other people. As we've already said, most adults who hurt others feel insecure and unsure of themselves deep inside. They may have become addicted to substances or activities. Perhaps they were hurt as children. Possibly they had inconsistent discipline that taught them to get what they want by manipulation. Because they didn't learn how to manage their feelings or actions, some turned into aggressors. They learned to bury their emotions and take the offensive to get what they want.

Angie could be the life of the party in some situations but abusive and angry in others. She was very cold to her former husband, who describes her this way.

> I think a lot has to do with Angie's mom and dad. She's used to getting her way. Her mom spoiled the hell out of her when she was a kid. Now, if it's not Angie's idea, it's a bad idea. She wants her way. She throws it out there right away that she's a bitch and you better do it her way or forget it. She'd tell you she's happy, but I don't buy it. She gripes about people all the time and calls them stupid morons.
>
> By listening to her stories, I'd say she could do too much as a kid. People who get their way their whole lives expect it. At sixteen years old she had a sweet ride, a Mustang. Shopping sprees. Top of the line. Spoiled. When I was raised we didn't have that stuff. She got her way. I think she got hit a lot, but her parents were lenient too. Her mother let her drink at parties. Her mom would always do whatever Angie wanted.

Inner weakness does not excuse behavior or diminish the harm it does, but understanding it can help you understand your TLO. When you recognize that your TLO's behavior comes from weakness rather than strength, you can deal with her more effectively and, maybe, with less fear and anger. It becomes easier to separate her actions and attitudes from her worth as a person—another part of letting go with love.

Denial

Denial is a defense mechanism people use to avoid painful thoughts or feelings by simply refusing to acknowledge them. Denial is a core problem for those addicted to drugs or alcohol and for other challenging loved ones, as well.

Denial is unconscious and can be very long lasting. It prevents people from taking control of their lives by blocking their awareness of their own actions, thoughts, and feelings. Denial often does allow them to avoid the pain of unwanted thoughts and emotions, but it does so at an even higher cost. It isolates people from their positive emotions and blocks emotional connections to other people.

HOW DID MY TLO GET THIS WAY?

Have you ever felt like walking up to your troubled loved one, thumping him on the head, and saying, "Hello! Anybody home?" Have you ever wanted to get up on your tiptoes and peek inside his brain to see what's going on in there? Well, we have news for you. You probably wouldn't find much that's all that different from what's going on in your own head.

That's why this section could also be titled, "How did *anybody* get this way?" Everyone has had struggles, problems, and setbacks. How is it that some people seem to do better than others in this game of life? Maybe you look at your own background and think, "I had it a lot worse than he did growing up. Why does he have so many more problems?"

The truth is, troubled people are often just as smart, caring, and well intended as you. But they seem to have an unending supply of conflicts and struggles, particularly with their closest relationships (like you, for example). Take a look at why that is.

Nature Versus Nurture

When trying to understand difficult adults, it can be useful to consider a long-standing debate in psychology called the "nature-nurture controversy." Put simply, the question is, "Are we humans the way we are because of nature (genetics or heredity) or nurture (early life experiences and environment)?" The prevailing opinion among psychotherapists seems to be that nurture contributes most to who we are.

If it is primarily nurture, what are the factors in early life that affect people? The following list gives some examples of early life influences.

- Parenting practices

- Siblings, especially older siblings

- Others living in the household

- Peers

- Teachers, coaches, and other authority figures

- Neighborhood

- Culture

- Religious or spiritual traditions

- Traumatic events

- Diet and nutrition

- Childhood illnesses, accidents, and birth complications

- Financial conditions

- Schools

Bobbi Lee talks about a friend of hers who is distant and has anger problems, which she believes stem from his home life.

His parents were cold. He was basically raised without love but in a very religious family. His father's father thought children should be seen and not heard. It's about upbringing. He's got a lot of anger in him. I think it's anger he never addressed because he was told Christians aren't supposed to get angry.

If people are largely a product of environment (nurture), as many who study human behavior believe, this is very good news indeed. It means all people can change the parts of themselves that they're not happy about. It means no one is a victim of genetics. Change is possible with hope, motivation, guidance, opportunity, and support.

Am I to Blame for My Son's or Daughter's Problems?—A Thought for Parents

Some parents might feel uncomfortable with what mental health professionals say about the effects of parenting practices. Sometimes parents feel guilty about how their children turned out. Many readers of this book may have an adult daughter or son who is the TLO they're thinking about as they read. Some probably blame themselves for their children's problems.

Maybe your spouse, former spouse, social workers, therapists, police, or authors have told you that you're to blame for your child's problems. But self-blame and guilt are neither deserved nor helpful. Your influence is just one of many. It is important—but it is still only one. Children do grow up, as you did. They become teenagers, young adults, adults, and senior citizens. Healthy adults take responsibility for their adult actions regardless of childhood experiences. See how Rick feels about his younger brother.

I really hate to say it, but my brother is just a punk kid. He's in prison at twenty-two. When we were kids, he broke into my room and stole my VCR. He stole from his own freaking family all the time. I had to have a lock on my door. The way he'd talk to my mom was awful—but then she'd feel bad, thinking she'd done something to make him mad. He got married real young, and he treated his wife bad, too. He didn't like the tone she had, and he'd read bad stuff into everything she said. Brand new newlyweds, and he wouldn't come home at night for his wife, and he had a new child at home. He's a mess. A wreck. And he's so young. That's the bad thing. We wonder what bloodline he comes from. Me and my sisters were never like that. My parents still beat themselves up about him. They think they did something wrong, but I don't think so. He's just a freak.

The best science and psychotherapy available cannot explain all human behavior. It probably never will. Sometimes you just don't know where your own or somebody else's behaviors come from.

The Newlyweds

There is a story of newlyweds who sat down for supper not long after their honeymoon. The young husband noticed that his wife had cut off both ends of the roast before she cooked it. He asked why, and she replied, "Well, I don't really know. That's the way Mom always did it."

Their curiosity aroused, they decided to ask her mother why it was done that way. A few days later, the bride asked, "Mom, Dave noticed I cut the ends off the roast the other night, and he wondered why. I don't really know why—I was just doing what you always did. Why do you cut the ends off?" To this her mother replied, "I guess I don't know, either, dear. My mother always did it that way."

Even more curious now, the young bride decided to ask her grandmother about it the next time they got together. That weekend, when she visited her grandmother, she brought up the question right away. "Grandmother, why did you always cut the ends off a roast before you cooked it?" "Well," replied her grandmother, "my roasting pan was too small."

As this story shows, some behaviors are passed down through the generations without anyone's knowing why they do them or where they came from.

So, if you harbor guilt for the parenting you've done, remember that many people and many life events have affected your grown daughter or son. You are not to blame. If you've made parenting decisions you regret, and they affect how you feel about yourself or how you interact with others today, consider getting counseling for yourself. That may help you work through your emotions. But let go of the guilt. It helps no one.

Childhood Experience Is a Factor, Not an Excuse

Childhood experiences are factors influencing who you are now. But those experiences are not an excuse for bad choices you make today. As an adult, you are 100 percent responsible for what you do. The same goes for your difficult loved one. How he was raised affected him, as did many other things, but now he's responsible for making his life what it can be.

How empowering! Your TLO is in control of what happens in his life. And you are in control of what happens in yours. Think about the newlyweds and their roast. That cooking practice touched three generations. Grandmother taught her daughter who taught her daughter who might have gone on to teach her own children the same thing if that young wife hadn't asked questions and made changes. As simple as this example is, it reminds us that we don't always know why we do the things we do, but we can change the things we do if we choose to.

Don't allow your TLO to blame you for his problems. Don't blame yourself, either. The blame game doesn't work for you or your troubled loved one. If you are to blame for your children's problems, who is to blame for yours? Your parents? If so, who is to blame for your parents' problems? Your grandparents? Then great-grandparents? Where does the blame stop?

Some troubled loved ones are masters at blaming others. Be careful not to fall into their traps. What happened in your child's younger years is a factor in his life, not an excuse.

SUMMING UP AND MOVING ON

In this chapter, we've looked at why troubling loved ones are the way they are. We hope that increases your understanding of your TLO. We hope that understanding has begun to diminish the anger, sadness, or guilt you might feel.

In these first three chapters as a whole, we've examined the behaviors of your troubled friend or relative, shed light on why they do what they do, and, hopefully, increased your own self-awareness.

As we move forward from here, we'll show you specific techniques for dealing successfully with your loved one. You'll learn to cope with your own thoughts, feelings, and actions to deal productively with the challenges you face. If your change improves things for your troublesome loved one, that's great. We hope it will, and it might. But your TLO's change is not our primary goal. Our primary goal is helping you change you—whether your TLO changes or not.

4

Let Go with Love

Janice's son, Jason, lives on the other side of town. He's always had one "bad break" after another—losing jobs, getting hooked up with unhealthy women, and getting arrested. He's been borrowing money from Janice for years and never pays her back. For her part, Janice feels guilty because she divorced his father when Jason was a teenager and hasn't been able to control him since. Now her own stress-related health problems are becoming serious. Finally Janice has begun to say no to her son, and here we see what happened the last time Jason came to ask his mother for money.

Jason let the door slam behind him as he left his mother's home and headed for his car. "This is bull," he muttered. "I'm never asking you for nothin' again." Back in the house, Janice began watering her plants. No more apologizing. No more crying. She was finally starting to accept that Jason was not the problem—she was.

Just then her oldest daughter called. "How are you, Mom?"

"I'm fine, honey," replied Janice.

"You don't sound so good. Has Jason been there?"

"Yes, Lisa. He just left. He's out of money again. But before you ask, I didn't give him any. I'm not doing that anymore. What everybody's been telling me is true. I gave in too much in the past, and now it's time for him to be a man and for me to let go of him. And I'm learning not to blame myself anymore."

"Wow! Good for you, Mom!" said Lisa. "I'm proud of you. You're doing the right thing."

"Thanks, Lisa. I'm learning. But now I'm sorry, but I have to go. I told the new neighbor I'd help her transplant those flowers in the back. I hope we can talk about this more later on." Just before she hung up, Janice said one last thing: "Lisa, I think Jason will be okay in the long run. I know I will."

Janice learned some important things about dealing with her troubling son. She's practicing a key concept of this book—how to let go with love. And now, you can, too.

LET GO WITH LOVE

To let go with love means to let go of trying to control the outcome of another person's actions. It means accepting that you can't control what other people do. It means accepting that you can only change yourself. For most people that's quite a challenge. This is the vital essence of letting go with love: you don't let go of *loving* your troublesome loved one. You let go of trying to *change* her.

Accepting your inability to control someone else sets you free. When you accept that other people are responsible for their own actions, you're no longer a victim of their requests, demands, and complaints. You might still decide to do things for your TLO, but that becomes a choice freely made, not something done from guilt, fear, or frustration.

When you let go with love you *choose* to do something—or not do something—for your difficult loved one. You also choose what you'll do for yourself, whether your troubled friend or relative likes it or not. This may sound selfish, but it isn't. Selfishness is defined as caring *only* about yourself *without regard* for the needs of others. Letting go with love is caring about *both* of you—without taking on her responsibilities.

Enmeshed, Disconnected, and Connected

To deal effectively with a difficult loved one and take care of yourself at the same time, you need to strike a balance between giving too much and giving too little. This means not trying desperately to fix your struggling loved one at one extreme—or cutting her out of your life at the other.

Let's take a look at the three ways that people interact with their troubled friends and relatives. They become: enmeshed (overinvolved), disconnected (underinvolved), or connected (healthfully involved).

ENMESHED

When you're enmeshed, you are overinvolved. You try too hard to fix the struggling person you love. You keep hoping she'll "get it," wake up, see the light, and become a responsible and caring citizen. You keep believing your special guidance and love will help her in ways others can't. You keep trying to change her, but it doesn't work.

Tony is a successful professional and loving father who has become enmeshed in the life of his adult daughter Allyson. She has a long-standing alcohol and drug problem. Tony's other two daughters are highly successful career women, which makes it even more difficult for him to stop rescuing Allyson.

> *I set up job interviews for Allyson several times, but she'd blow it every time. She doesn't really want to work, but it took me a long time to figure that out. I sent her to a private inpatient treatment program that cost me $35,000. She's still using today. She's been living in a hotel room for months now, and I often pay for it. But I pay it directly to the hotel because she'd spend it on drugs and booze. There's something wrong when you can't attend well to your own marriage, job, or yourself because you're thinking about somebody else. It's a problem if someone else's life is constantly on your mind instead of your own.*

Lots of people have difficulty seeing their own behavior as an attempt to change their difficult loved one. They say they're just trying to help. Just giving a little nudge. But anything you do hoping your TLO will think or act differently is an attempt to change her. Even changing yourself with the hopes she will change because of it is *an attempt to change her*. It doesn't work. That's enmeshment.

Here are examples of what you might hear from enmeshed friends or relatives (or yourself?) about a troubling loved one. "I've got to keep trying." "Why doesn't she love me?" "What am I doing wrong?" "He's too confused (abused, innocent, upset, addicted, and so on) to do the right thing, so I've got to do it for him." "I'm strong enough to take the hurt."

DISCONNECTED

Being disconnected is the opposite of being enmeshed. A disconnected individual refuses to engage with his TLO in any meaningful way. He may even cut that difficult relative or friend out of his life.

Some people disconnect from others because they've been deeply hurt, and others do so because their usual tendency is to pull away from all difficult relationships. Either way, their disconnectedness reflects their emotional pain and struggles with a very challenging situation.

Here's what you might hear from a disconnected person talking about his TLO. "The hell with him. He won't listen to me, so I'm through with him." "She can stop trying to get on my good side. I'm done with her." "I don't care." "If he changes his ways and wakes up, I'll think about it. Until then, I'm through."

CONNECTED

When you're connected, you find a healthy balance between over-involvement (enmeshed) and underinvolvement (disconnected). You don't give away your own valuable time, money, or emotional energy like the enmeshed person does. You don't shut off your emotions like the disconnected person does. You find a middle ground where you stay involved with your TLO, but you decide where, when, and how that happens.

Connected adults might be heard saying, "It hurts me deeply to see him do this over and over, but I know I can't change him." "I'm going to take care of me." "I'm not dropping out of her life *or* giving up my life to her." All these statements express the connected adult's desire to care about himself and his troubled loved one.

Am I Enmeshed, Disconnected, or Connected?

How are you handling your TLO? Do you think you're enmeshed, disconnected, or connected? Are you doing too much? Are you doing too little? Or are you splitting it down the middle?

The following exercise will give you a better understanding of how enmeshed, disconnected, or connected you are. Circle the "T" at the end of each statement that is true for you, and circle the "F" for each statement that is false for you. (If you have more than one TLO, take the quiz for each of them.)

	True	False
1. I sometimes volunteer to do things for my TLO but resent it later.	T	F
2. I've cut my difficult loved one out of my life for long periods of time.	T	F
3. If my TLO yells at me, I end the conversation rather than be abused.	T	F
4. I feel unappreciated by my troublesome loved one.	T	F
5. I refuse to speak to my crazy-making relative or friend.	T	F
6. I do things for my TLO out of love, not guilt.	T	F
7. I feel used by my problematic friend or relative.	T	F
8. I will not discuss my TLO with anyone.	T	F
9. I know I'm not responsible for her actions.	T	F

10. I work harder at fixing his problems than he does.	T	F
11. I've decided not to send cards or presents to my TLO ever again.	T	F
12. I am free to enjoy myself.	T	F
13. I sometimes get so upset about my TLO that I can't eat or sleep.	T	F
14. I no longer have feelings for her.	T	F
15. I refuse to make excuses for my TLO.	T	F
16. I'm so stressed by my TLO that I'm having health problems.	T	F
17. My TLO no longer affects my life in any way.	T	F
18. I have a right to happiness even when my TLO is unhappy.	T	F
19. I sometimes make excuses for my TLO.	T	F
20. I refuse to look at my TLO.	T	F
21. I feel little or no resentment when I give things to my TLO.	T	F
22. I feel responsible for his problems.	T	F
23. I couldn't care less what that crazy-maker does.	T	F
24. I'm not embarrassed by my TLO's actions.	T	F
25. I often do things for her because I feel bad if I don't.	T	F
26. I know he doesn't care about me.	T	F
27. I refuse to be manipulated by my troublesome loved one.	T	F
28. I lose my temper with my TLO too often.	T	F
29. I've been told I shouldn't be so stubborn with my TLO.	T	F
30. I ask for what I want from my TLO but don't demand to get it.	T	F

SCORING

Circle the numbers in the table below that correspond with the statements you marked as true in the list above. Count how many true answers you have circled in each column and write the total at the bottom.

A Enmeshed	B Disconnected	C Connected
1	2	3
4	5	6
7	8	9
10	11	12
13	14	15
16	17	18
19	20	21
22	23	24
25	26	27
28	29	30
Total _____	Total _____	Total _____

Column A contains the statements that indicate an enmeshed style of interacting with your problematic relative or friend. Column B statements indicate a disconnected style, and column C indicates a connected style. The higher your total at the bottom of any column, the more you use that style of interacting with your TLO. Your highest score shows the interaction style you use most often.

Scores from 0 to 2 in any column indicate low use of that style. Scores of 3 or 4 indicate moderate use. Scores of 5 and above indicate a heavy reliance on that type of interaction with your difficult loved one.

A high enmeshed score indicates you give of yourself too much and don't have enough emotional independence from your TLO. A high disconnected score indicates you may have separated too much from your troublesome relative or friend. This distancing is understandable, but it may hurt both of you more than you realize. A high score in the connected style indicates you have the ability to balance your needs with your TLO's.

How Do I Relate to My Troubled Loved One?

Most people have one dominant style of relating to their troublesome loved ones, but they occasionally use one or both of the other styles as well. A variety of circumstances affects how you respond to your TLO. Your style might change in response to your TLO's specific problems; or, if you have more than one difficult loved one, you may relate to each one differently. Your approach is also affected by the level of support you get from others and how well your own life is going.

Enmeshment limits you and your difficult loved one for a variety of reasons, including the exhaustion it creates in you and the irresponsibility it encourages in her. Being disconnected from your TLO limits you both in many ways, including isolation and the potential for permanent separation.

A connected style takes the middle road. With connectedness you're much less likely to harbor anger, guilt, or fear. With connectedness you maintain a relationship with your TLO, but you decide how you interact with her, and you take care of yourself throughout.

To gain more insight about yourself, use the lines below to respond to this question (if you have more than one TLO, answer it for each): "What has the quiz I just completed taught me about how I relate to my difficult relative or friend?"

Based upon what you've learned in this book, the views of people you trust, and your own intuition, circle the word below that best describes your primary way of relating to your troublesome loved one:

Enmeshed   *Connected*   *Disconnected*

Use the lines below to write two or three things you often do that demonstrate your enmeshed, disconnected, or connected behavior. Doing so will help you get a clearer understanding of how you interact with your TLO. Begin by completing this sentence: "I think I am enmeshed (or) disconnected (or) connected because I . . ."

_____

_____

_____

A THREE-STEP PROCESS FOR LETTING GO WITH LOVE

Below is a three-step process for dealing with your unhealthy reactions to your TLO. Use this process every time you find yourself over-reacting or underreacting to your difficult loved one. This includes rescuing or abandoning him. It means reacting with negative or demeaning thoughts about yourself or him, and it means being extremely bothered by guilt, anger, or fear. The three steps of letting go with love are: Feel it, Think it, Act it.

Step 1. Feel it. Acknowledge and accept your thoughts and feelings.

Step 2. Think it. Rethink what happened and plan how you'll respond.

Step 3. Act it. Replace your old behaviors with new ones.

It may take a bit of practice to carry out this new way of dealing with old behaviors and beliefs, but it can be done. Your old way of reacting has been with you a long time, and change takes a while. You're not just changing behaviors, either. You're also grappling with the strong feelings attached to those old behaviors.

There will be times when you know exactly which course of action is the best one to take with your problematic person but feel too upset to do it. This is a common reaction to strong emotions, so don't be discouraged. Keep working on the changes you want to make. Let's look at the three-step let-go-with-love process in more detail.

Step 1: Feel It. Acknowledge and Accept Your Feelings

In this first step, you acknowledge your feelings. Acknowledge them directly by saying to yourself something like, "It hurts so much when she doesn't return my calls," or "I feel so guilty about what I've done," or "I'm very worried about her."

This doesn't mean you wallow in painful feelings. It means you acknowledge them and move on. Your difficult emotions are with you whether you admit them or not, so give them voice to set them free. If you deny them, they don't go away—they go underground. Then they resurface as headaches, stomachaches, low energy, and lost sleep.

This step of acknowledging difficult feelings may seem like the exact wrong thing to do. Many people spend their entire lives trying to avoid difficult feelings. But allowing your feelings to be "heard" is absolutely necessary. And don't fear that acknowledging your powerful emotions will make them worse. In fact, the exact opposite is true. Denying them and trying to force them out of your mind without acknowledging and working through them gives powerful emotions their staying power. If you don't acknowledge your feelings, they'll continually bubble up in the most inconvenient ways.

Step 2: Think It. Rethink What Happened and Plan How You'll React

In step 2, you reinterpret the incident that occurred and then plan a different reaction so you're ready the next time you start feeling or acting in your old way. The following suggestions can help you deal with your situation. And be aware that there are no absolute right or wrong ways to do this. Try the ideas that fit for you. If you come up with additional ideas that work, use them.

TAKE A DEEP BREATH

Prepare to rethink what happened by taking two or three deep breaths. This clears the head and calms the heart, and can be helpful any time you feel anxious or upset. Standing, sitting, or lying still, very slowly breathe in and out. Close your eyes if you wish, and calmly tell yourself you are relaxing.

TALK TO YOURSELF

Now have a little talk with yourself, out loud or in your head. Analyze what just happened with your TLO. Who did what? How did you feel? What were you thinking? Tell yourself you want to do things differently.

QUESTION YOUR OLD BELIEFS

Challenge your automatic responses that say you have to react a certain way. Examples of automatic responses are: being artificially nice to a TLO right after he says something mean; making phone calls for an adult to cover for her; and telling your TLO what she should do.

If you do find automatic responses coming to you, ask yourself questions to challenge them: "Why *should* I be nice to her when she's mean to me?" "Why *am* I working so hard to fix this problem when he doesn't even seem to care?" "What makes me think *I* know what she needs?" "Who *says* I have to feel bad because he feels bad?"

To help you notice your own automatic responses, focus on a recent situation involving your TLO in which you reacted in ways that didn't feel good. For example, maybe your TLO borrowed money from someone and you were unhappy about it, yet you stayed silent; or your TLO and his children live in a very cluttered and dirty apartment and you have, yet again, gone over there to clean up their mess.

Once you have a situation in mind, write two or three beliefs about your TLO or yourself that affected what you did in that situation.

_____

_____

_____

Now take each of your beliefs individually and use the space below, or your journal, to address the following questions: "Have my reactions worked for me, my TLO, and others?" "Where do my beliefs come from?" "Are my beliefs true?" "How do my thoughts or actions stop me from getting what I want?"

_____

_____

_____

==

REMEMBER TIMES YOU'VE DONE WELL

As you continue in step 2, think back to times you have handled troubling situations well. Recall them in detail. If you have trouble with this, imagine what would have been the best way to handle that situation, or think of what others have suggested you do at times like that.

Focus on the solutions that make the most sense to you. If you want additional ideas, think of someone who is compassionate and wise. It may be the person you thought of on the wisdom ladder from chapter 3. Think about what she has said or would say if you asked her.

COME UP WITH A NEW PLAN

An important part of step 2 is coming up with a specific plan for doing things differently in the future. Throw out old constricting beliefs and develop a creative plan of action. Think of all the things you could do differently. In your journal, generate a list of new ways to respond.

Generate your list by remembering things that have worked, even slightly, in the past. Do a brainstorming session in which you write down ideas as they come, off the top of your head. Consider your new ideas while taking a brisk walk that will energize your mind. Ask trusted people in your life for their thoughts. When you do generate new ideas, give them a chance to grow in your mind. Don't judge them as stupid or impossible. Think of reasons they will work rather than reasons they won't.

Continuing in your journal, plan exactly what you're going to do instead of reacting in your old way. As soon as you realize you're in an uncomfortable situation with your TLO, start talking to yourself in your mind. Tell yourself you want to resolve this situation successfully. Tell yourself that you may not be able to control your TLO but you can control how you react. Remind yourself to stay calm. Think about how you can take care of yourself. Think about what a trusted and wise friend would do.

Then combine those thoughts, and come to a conclusion. Tell yourself what you think is the best way to continue. Be specific. Say, for example, "Now that John has yelled at me, I'll leave the house if he starts yelling at me again." Another example would be to pull your thoughts together and tell yourself, "Uncle Pete is drunk and angry. If he decides to drive his daughter home, I will warn him that I'll call the police." Then follow through with your decision.

Once you've decided what action you'll take, repeat it to yourself as often as you need to. This will reinforce your commitment to your plan. If you have time and wish to do it, write your plan down and look at it when you need a reminder.

Here's an example. Let's say your adult daughter yells at her child a lot and that your standard response is to smile serenely at your daughter. In addition, you take out your frustration with her by not talking to your husband. Using step 2, take a deep breath and pull your plan together. It might be, for example, to calmly tell your daughter you feel upset when she raises her voice. To finish this step, talk directly with your husband about your problem with your daughter. Ask for his support and encouragement so you can enjoy the rest of your day together.

Step 3: Act It. Replace Your Old Behaviors with New Ones

Now it's time to carry out the plan you made in step 2. If you've told yourself you'll get busy with a task when you find yourself worrying about your TLO, get busy with something. If you've decided you're going to excuse yourself and leave the room every time your father makes nasty comments to your mother, make sure you do leave.

One tool to help you carry out your plan is to imagine yourself completing it. Visualize yourself politely excusing yourself from your father, turning around, and walking out. See a "movie" of this in your head. If it helps, play the "movie" over and over before you see him. You can do this visualization for any changes you want to make.

Remember, your plans won't work unless you do them. So bite the bullet. Take the plunge. Face your fears—and carry out your plan. Usually it's hardest to do this the first time or two, but don't give up. It gets easier.

APPLYING LET GO WITH LOVE

To help you get a better idea of how to let go with love, we'll illustrate the process with this chapter's opening story about Janice and her TLO, her son, Jason. The story tells about the excellent progress Janice made in dealing differently with Jason. He had been angry and irresponsible for years. He frequently dated unhealthy women, lost jobs, and borrowed money from Janice.

Janice used the three steps of letting go with love as they are outlined below to change how she dealt with her son. If you wish, go back and reread Janice's story now.

Let's look behind the scenes at Janice's thought process as she developed a new way to respond to her son. To begin her change, Janice started with the first part of step 1, "Feel it." She chose a common behavior of her son's that she greatly disliked—his borrowing money from her. She also described what she usually did when Jason asked for money: "Whenever Jason has asked for money, I've given it to him— even when I didn't want to." Then she described how she felt when she gave him money: "I felt terrible. At first I felt guilty because he had so many problems, then I got afraid of what he'd do if I didn't give him money. Afterwards, I'd be mad at myself for giving in again."

For step 2, "Think it," Janice reinterpreted what happened when her son asked for money. She said, "I thought I was supposed to give him money because that's what moms do. I thought it was my responsibility to help him no matter what. Now I look at it differently. When he asks for money I don't have to give it to him. I can say no to him." Then Janice developed a plan for what she would do differently the next time Jason asked for money. She stated her plan like this: "When Jason asks for money, I'm straight out going to say no because nothing else works with him. I expect he'll be mad, but I'm going to stick to my guns. If I need somebody to talk to afterwards to make me feel better, I'll call my daughter."

In step 3, Janice reduced her plan of action to a statement she could remember: "When Jason asks for money I'm saying no, and calling my daughter if I need support."

Changing How You Respond

You've read how Janice used the three-step process for letting go with love. Use the following lines, or your journal, to work out a new way of responding to a common interaction you have with your TLO.

_____

STEP 1: FEEL IT

Write down a behavior your difficult loved one often does, one you don't like and that you overreact or underreact to.

_____

_____

_____

Next, write a description of what you do when he does that. You might start this description with "When my TLO does (write the behavior from above), I react by …

_____

_____

_____

Next, whatever feelings you go through at that time—guilt, anger, fear, hopelessness, or others—acknowledge them and write them here. Start with "I feel ...

_____

_____

_____

STEP 2: THINK IT

This step has two parts.

Rethink. The first is to develop new ways of interpreting what happened with your TLO. To do this, challenge your old ways of thinking. Examine any assumptions you might have about what you "should" or "shouldn't" do in that situation. Ask yourself if your thoughts are accurate and helpful or a result of habit or fear. Ask yourself how others you respect would interpret the situation if they were in your shoes. What would they do? On the lines below, write one or two new ways of interpreting what happened.

_____

_____

_____

Plan. The second part of this step is to develop a specific plan of what you'll do next time a similar situation comes up. To do this, ask yourself what a firm but fair way of reacting would be. Think of what a wise friend would do in your situation. Think of how you would react if you were not worried about your TLO's reaction.

Write your plan on the lines below. Be specific. You might say, for example, "The next time Mom ignores me when I talk to her, I'll say, 'Mom, please say something when I talk to you.'" Another example might be, "When my brother takes over a conversation with stories about himself, I will politely excuse myself and leave."

_____

_____

_____

STEP 3: ACT IT

Carry out your new plan of action. Write a statement to yourself committing to follow through with your new plan. It might be something like, "I promise myself I will follow through with my new plan the next time my son gets into an argument with his father."

_____

_____

_____

_____

Use these three steps to help you let go with love in any interaction with your troublesome loved one. And in all those situations, remember that your main goal is to decide for yourself what your involvement with your TLO will be like. You want to make sure that she does not take advantage of you and that you have a good life even if your TLO can not or will not take care of herself.

A Few More Thoughts About Enmeshment

Sometimes it's very difficult to let go with love. No one can predict exactly what will happen when you do. You may have been enmeshed with or disconnected from your TLO for years, and it's frightening to change long-standing, habitual responses to someone you care about. Even so, such changes make it more likely that your loved one will see his or her own problems and that you'll have a calmer life.

Here's an example of enmeshment that changed into healthy, connected interaction. Christine had helped raise her four grandchildren. She and her son, the children's dad, did everything they could to raise the kids well. Looking back, Christine sees that she often took on more responsibility for her grandchildren's mistakes than she should have. She realized that her actions actually contributed to her oldest grandson, TJ, avoiding responsibility for his own life.

> *It's bad. They all grew up knowing what's right and wrong, but, oh, my God, TJ just keeps getting in deeper and deeper. Somehow he grew up never knowing there was a punishment. If he got into trouble in school, he'd always get out of it somehow. I tried to steer him in the right direction, but I don't think I helped any. When he was younger, all he had to do was look at me with those big beautiful eyes of his, and I'd ease up on him. But now I know that wasn't good for him.*
>
> *Even though he's grown up, he still comes to me, but I don't do things the way I used to. I tell him to stand on his own two feet. I tell him I'll help a little, but I won't do for him anymore. He doesn't want to hear that from me. One day he's going to call and say, "I'm in jail, Gran" and I'm going to say, "I'm sorry to hear that, sweetie." I know I can't help him. I just can't do it. How sad is that, 'cause I love him to death. Hopefully some day he'll come around.*

If frequently giving in to people isn't good for them, what do you do instead? How do you show others you care without doing too much for them? An illustration from the work world might help. Let's say you're an accountant. Clients come to you to get their taxes done, do their books, etc. You are responsible for treating them with respect and handling their finances thoroughly and legally. You are not responsible if they don't bring you all the information you asked for or if they engage in illegal activities without your knowledge. You are not responsible if they lose their jobs or families. You might feel badly for them if they fall on hard times, and you might feel angry or frustrated if they don't deal honestly with you—but the results of their choices are not your responsibility.

The same goes for your troublesome relative or friend. You can care and offer reasonable assistance, but her choices are hers. There's a saying that when you care more about a problem than the person who has the problem, you are part of the problem.

What do you do if your TLO gets himself or others into truly dangerous situations? What is your responsibility then? What do you do when there are children in the picture? It certainly isn't their fault they have a messed up mom or dad. Well, as difficult and even harsh as it may sound, the fact is that enmeshment is still enmeshment, and it still only postpones the inevitable.

At some point, every human being needs to learn that when they act, there are consequences. It's just a fact of this world. If you walk out in front of a speeding car, you will get hurt. If you drink too much, you'll get drunk. When you ignore or yell at people for long enough, they might become ill or go away. Not wanting these difficult facts to be true doesn't keep them from being true.

We urge you to step back and look at your choices regarding the help you offer your loved one. Handle your own problems, and let her handle hers. You can't be a buffer between her actions and her consequences forever—but even if you could, you wouldn't be helping. The sooner she learns to handle her own struggles and successes, the sooner she'll learn to be a responsible adult. And the sooner you'll be able to find peace for yourself.

WHO CAN I CHANGE?

As we've said several times already, an unpleasant reality about changing others is that you can't. It doesn't work. It doesn't matter if your TLO is a liar, a cheat, abused or confused, a silent victim, or total crazy-maker. You can't change him.

The awfulness of this is that it's true. And the beauty of this is that it's true. It's beautiful because accepting this truth frees you from feeling responsible for other people's choices.

In the next chapter we'll look at additional thoughts on letting go with love. To end this one, we leave you with the Serenity Prayer, written in 1943 by Reinhold Niebuhr. It can guide you through tough times, as it has guided countless others.

> *God, grant me the serenity to accept the things I cannot change,*
> *The courage to change the things I can,*
> *And the wisdom to know the difference.*

This is another version of the Serenity Prayer. It speaks to much of what has been said in this chapter and book.

> *God, grant me the serenity to accept the people I cannot change,*
> *The courage to change who I can,*
> *And the wisdom to know it's me.*

5

Communicating with Your Troublesome Loved One

Communication can make or break a relationship. In this story about Nick and his son, Kyle, we see that anger, once expressed, is hard to take back. But Nick does a good job of looking at himself and expressing his true feelings once he has a chance to calm down.

"Kyle, you can't do that! How can you even think about quitting that job?" Kyle's father, Nick, was furious. He tried to keep his voice down because the whole family was in his backyard celebrating Father's Day. But his son was quitting his fifth job in as many years. Now red in the face, Nick growled, "What about your family? Don't you care about them at all? Don't you give a damn about anybody but yourself?!"

Kyle responded in kind. "You should talk. All you think about is money. You don't care about my family or me! I don't give a damn about money, and I don't give a damn about you!" Kyle stormed out to the backyard, where he tried to act like nothing was wrong.

Nick battled with his emotions. Angry with his son, and now embarrassed by his own behavior, he paced and thought. Slowly, his anger subsided, and he began thinking more clearly. He went outside to Kyle, who was smoking a cigarette away from the others. Nick looked him in the eye, but with love this time instead of anger. Nick began to speak. "Son, I'm sorry. I blew up at you because of my own worries. I was wrong. I've got to stop trying to control you. You have your own life now, and I've got to realize that. I'm sorry I lost my temper."

Tears welled up in Kyle's eyes. Nick hugged his son. This felt good. Nick and Kyle had always wanted this closeness, but it was often difficult to feel. Troubled decisions and strong emotions often got in the way. But things definitely felt good right then.

It's hard to tell who might be the troublesome loved one in this story—Kyle, who can't hold a job, or his dad, who can't hold his temper. But Nick's way of relating to his son offers us two distinctly different methods—confrontational and caring. In Nick's first exchange with his son, his emotions outran his mouth. He swore, yelled, and blamed Kyle while telling him what was "wrong" with him. After settling his own emotions, Nick stopped blaming Kyle. He told Kyle what was going on inside himself and admitted his own errors. It's pretty clear which approach drew them closer.

COMMUNICATION THAT WORKS

This chapter is about communicating with your troubling loved one. Communication is a huge part of any relationship—an invisible link between people that transmits each one's thoughts and feelings. The ways in which we employ that communication link can move us closer together or keep us further apart.

Communication is part skill, part art. It is learned from our parents and other caregivers as we grow up and is affected by the choices we make as adults. It's highly complex on one hand and amazingly simple on the other.

As long as you express yourself in a respectful way, you always have the right to say what you think. When you tell your truth respectfully you are not responsible for other people's reactions or feelings. They are. If they overreact, it's their responsibility. If they're hurt or angry, they are responsible for dealing with their feelings. This is true of all the people in your life.

There may be times when you have to say things that others don't want to hear. Difficult things happen in life, and sometimes difficult truths have to be told. This is part of human existence, pure and simple.

But you have a choice in *how* you tell those difficult truths. You can be aggressive and disrespectful or speak assertively and respectfully.

The goal of healthy communication is to say your truth honestly and assertively, even when others don't like what you say. If you don't speak up, you can become a victim, keeping the truth to yourself out of fear. Manipulative people thrive on that. If you allow yourself to believe you're responsible for their feelings, they'll fault you for everything. And why wouldn't they? If you don't stand up for yourself, you give them permission to blame you.

A Caution

In some cases, aggressive TLOs physically harm others. If someone you care about has that potential, it's best not to speak your mind unless you're in a safe place. That could mean involving police, lawyers, family, mental health professionals, or others.

Dealing with physically aggressive loved ones by involving others is in itself a form of assertiveness. In this assertiveness you consciously choose not to confront them. Whenever possible, avoid all interactions, assertive or otherwise, with an aggresive TLO, unless you feel safe.

Examine Your Own Thoughts and Feelings

You need to be aware of your own thoughts and feelings before you'll be able to successfully communicate with your TLO. They might be strong, and if you aren't aware of them they're likely to keep you from achieving your goals.

Before you begin a conversation with your difficult loved one, examine your own thoughts and feelings. Do you feel hurt? Scared? Guilty? Angry? Disgusted? Depressed? Are you holding a grudge? Are you looking at your mistakes, too? Are you being open-minded?

Take a moment to write in the space below the emotions you experience most when you're talking with your TLO. Then write down common thoughts you have when you talk with your TLO.

Give Up the Fantasy That Your Difficult Loved One Will Get It

When you see someone you love making serious mistakes over and over, it's quite natural to want him to make better decisions. As a result, you might often find yourself trying to get him to agree with you, admit his mistakes, or apologize for what he's done.

Stop waiting for him to see the light. If he isn't ready yet, that's just how it is, no matter how well you express yourself. Give up the fantasy that your TLO is going to say, "Oh, my God, you're right. I see what you're saying now. You were right all along."

Angela tried for years to change her husband, who was emotionally distant. It took her a long time to realize she couldn't.

Warren wasn't engaged in anything I was doing. I'd try to get him involved in going places with me, but he wouldn't respond. I drove out of state for all these weddings and two funerals, and he didn't go. People I knew for years didn't even know we were married. After a while, in a way, I was hiding it because I didn't want them to know. He wouldn't talk to anyone or relate to them. He went to nothing I did. Zero. We're divorced now.

Angela finally let go of her belief that Warren would become involved in her life. Ultimately she chose to divorce him. That may or may not be the option you would choose. You could, for example, decide to stay with him but develop your own life, with the understanding that he will not be part of it in certain ways. But any choice works best when you give up the fantasy that you can change your TLO. Accept him for who he is, protect yourself from his actions whenever necessary, and do your best to love him. Then go ahead and enjoy this day that is yours.

PASSIVE, ASSERTIVE, AGGRESSIVE

When people get into difficult conversations with troublesome friends and relatives, they tend to respond in one of two ways. They either passively accept what their TLO says and does, or they aggressively argue or fight.

People in passive mode don't say what they're thinking, and others take advantage of them. Although passive people often appear happy and helpful, on the inside they're angry. They're angry because they aren't getting what they want—and they aren't getting what they want because they don't ask. Passive people are often afraid they'll say the wrong thing, be overpowered, or hurt someone's feelings—so they clam up.

When people are aggressive, they speak their mind but with too much anger and too little listening. They're pushy or manipulative in their attempts to make others do what they think is right. They don't take no for an answer. They appear angry on the outside but are very afraid on the inside. Frustrated with their inability to make their TLO do what they think is right, they sometimes blow up.

There is another choice—assertiveness. Assertive people speak their truth. They ask for what they want in respectful ways, without demanding to get it. They speak up openly and calmly, without clamming up in fear or blowing up in anger.

Clam Up, Blow Up, Speak Up

It's not unusual for people to be passive most of the time and aggressive every once in a while. In this pattern, people hold back from expressing themselves as long as they can, until they finally lose their cool. They hold back because they aren't sure how to safely express their strong feelings. Unable to keep their thoughts to themselves any longer, they explode. This is called "clam up—clam up—clam up—blow up."

Several specific clues in your behavior will tell you when you're clamming up (passive), blowing up (aggressive), or speaking up (assertive). This section will help you identify these clues so you can decide which way you want to conduct yourself. Let's take a look at the clues for each of the three types of expression.

Clam Up

You are passive when you do any of the following:

- You think of what you want to say to your TLO, but you clam up out of fear you'll blow up, say the wrong thing, or set him off.

- You do things for your TLO but resent her because she doesn't acknowledge what you do, or she takes advantage of you.

Blow Up

You are aggressive when you do any of the following:

- Swear

- Yell

- Call names

- Give the cold shoulder or silent treatment

- Threaten

- Use physical force of any kind to control your TLO (grab, hit, push, hold against his will, pull hair, block his exit, damage his possessions)

Speak Up

You are assertive when you do either of the following:

- Tell people what you think and how you feel without demanding they agree

- Ask for what you want without demanding to get it

Most of us have a primary way of expressing ourselves with our TLO but react in other ways on some occasions. A common example would be someone who is usually passive but can also be aggressive or assertive. You might, for example, be assertive with your husband but passive with a boss. You may be passive with your TLO a great deal of the time but suddenly become aggressive out of the blue.

To improve how you respond to those around you, learn to recognize which mode you're in at any given time. This exercise can help you do that. Complete the sentences below. Refer to the explanations of passive, aggressive, and assertive behavior above to help you identify your own behavior.

I can tell I'm usually (circle one) passive assertive aggressive with my TLO because I usually react with the following thoughts and actions:

_____

_____

_____

Think now of one specific time you reacted to your TLO in the mode you circled above. Use the lines below to write a brief description of that incident.

_____

_____

_____

Now write what you said or did during that incident which indicated you were being passive, assertive, or aggressive.

_____

_____

_____

Think now about how you felt after that incident was over. Think about how you would have felt if you had been more assertive. Compare the two feelings on the lines below.

_____

_____

_____

Describe here what you could have done to be more assertive and less passive or aggressive.

_____

_____

_____

Speak Your Truth

If you're angry with someone, tell her so. If you want to be thanked for something you've done, ask to be thanked. If you don't want to do something for your TLO, say so. If you want time to yourself, ask for it. It's your right and responsibility to speak up.

As you speak up, remember you're speaking *your* truth, not *the* truth. This is particularly helpful to remember if you're angry or upset. Your troublesome relative or friend has her *own* truth—her own view of the situation, her feelings and opinions. That's okay. Speaking your truth is not about being "right." It is not about her doing what you want. It is about assertively expressing yourself so you can let go of bothersome thoughts and move on.

If, for example, your TLO tells you "You hate me. I can tell," he may believe that, but it doesn't make it so. Go ahead and speak your truth. You might say something like, "I don't like it when you tell me how I feel. My feelings are mine, and I don't hate you."

As another example, let's say your difficult loved one insists, "You've got to come over here right now. I have to go to work, and I've got nobody to watch the kids." You can respond with something like "I'm sorry you've got no one to babysit, but it doesn't work for me to do that right now. I'm sorry, but I can't help you." There are two different truths here: his and yours. Yours may not be the only truth, but it is important for you to say it regardless of what your TLO says.

Here is a way to know you're speaking your truth assertively and appropriately without intending to hurt people's feelings: say what's on your mind without swearing, yelling, name-calling, threatening, or using type of physical force. Following this guideline, and the following information about I-messages, you can speak up confidently. You can tell people what you believe and how you feel. You can ask for what you want, knowing their response is their responsibility.

I-MESSAGES AND YOU-MESSAGES

You've learned how to identify when you're being passive, assertive, or aggressive. You know that clamming up and blowing up get you nowhere. You know that assertiveness works and that speaking assertively means you won't swear, yell, call names, threaten, or use physical force.

Now we'll look at specific language you can use to speak assertively. Effective communication includes what are called I-messages, which tell other people about you—how you feel, what you think, and what you want. Unfortunately, many people too often use another type of communication—you-messages. Instead of telling the listener about what's going on with you, you-messages tell the listener what you think is wrong with him.

You-Messages

You-messages tend to be critical or blaming. They feed hurt and fear and set up the listener to respond defensively. You-messages sound like this: "You aren't listening to me," "You're driving me nuts with all this noise," "You just don't understand me," or "Don't you ever do what you say you're going to do?"

I-Messages

I-messages, on the other hand, are empowering and positive. They don't threaten or attack the other person. They support compassion and listening. They help the listener pay better attention and ask questions. I-messages are useful for starting conversations and creating closeness.

I-messages are extremely helpful in starting discussions on difficult topics and are very helpful throughout conversations. Keep your I-messages brief. The fewer details you include, the less there is for your TLO to argue about. Do your best to clearly establish what you want and maintain that as a primary focus of the discussion. I-messages sound like this: "I'm frustrated about this job not being done." "I'm feeling afraid right now." "I'm upset about the suspicious tone I hear."

Many times, I-messages express your feelings of sadness, fear, or upset (as in the examples above), as well as anger, frustration, disappointment, and so on. Sharing how you feel is very effective and tells the most about you. You can feel confident sharing in this way because it is your truth, not just an opinion. If, for example, you change the blaming you-message "You aren't listening to me" to an I-message such as "I'm sad about what's going on between us," your TLO is less likely to be defensive, and you'll feel confident that what you're saying is true.

I-MESSAGES HAVE THREE PARTS

I-messages convey three pieces of information about the speaker: how you feel, what you're upset about, and what you want. Let's look at them one at a time.

`How you feel.` In this first part of the I-message, you tell your challenging loved one what emotions you're experiencing. Let him know if you're sad, angry, fearful, happy, or whatever. Examples of feeling statements are "I'm sad about something," or "I'm kind of scared to tell you this." Don't confuse feelings with thoughts. Examples of thoughts are "I think you aren't fair to me," or "I don't like what you said." Don't include your thoughts about the other person in your I-messages.

`What you're upset about.` In this second part of the I-message, you very briefly tell the listener what you're reacting to. Examples might be "You said you'd be home at 6:00, and now it's 8:30," or "I asked three times this week to talk to you about something, and we still haven't done it."

What you want. Here you state what you want. Examples are "I'd appreciate a call if you're coming home late," or "I'd like you to put down what you're doing and talk with me about this."

PUTTING IT ALL TOGETHER

Combining the three parts of an I-message makes for a brief and effective statement that is assertive without blaming. See how they combine in the next two examples of effective I-messages.

Example 1:

How you feel:	I'm angry about something right now.
What you're upset about:	You said you'd be home by 6:00, and it's now 8:30.
What you want:	I'd appreciate a call if you're coming home late.

Example 2:

How you feel:	I'm kind of scared to tell you this,
What you're upset about:	but I've asked three times this week to talk to you about something, and we still haven't talked.
What you want:	I'd like you to put down what you're doing and talk about this with me.

You have every right to tell people how you feel, what you're upset about, and what you want. That isn't bossy, silly, or selfish. It's reasonable, honest, and direct. As long as you speak up but don't swear, call names, yell, threaten, or use any physical force, you are expressing yourself assertively and appropriately.

Use the space below to write and practice an I-message you will use in response to your TLO's frustrating behavior. Choose a behavior that is relatively minor yet likely to happen again. Include all three parts in your I-message. The sentence structure below might help.

1. I feel a bit (an emotion like hurt, sad, happy, or scared) right now ...

2. because (what happened) ...

3. and I would like (in simple terms, tell her what you want) ...

1. _____

2. _____

3. _____

Practice your I-message out loud to yourself several times. See how it sounds. Adapt it until you're more comfortable with the sound of it. Ask someone close to you if they'll listen to your I-message and tell you what they like and dislike about it. Then try your I-message on your TLO. Remember that your I-message is a work in progress. It might be imperfect, but even if you state only one or two elements of the I-message in the beginning, that's a great start. Keep working with I-messages, and they'll soon feel more natural.

SEVEN SUPER SUGGESTIONS FOR BETTER COMMUNICATION

When communicating with your TLO, *how* and *when* you say things can be as important as *what* you say. The seven super suggestions listed

here will help you speak up assertively with your difficult loved one—
and others.

Allow Emotions to Cool

Don't talk about difficult subjects with your TLO when either of
you is angry. Strong feelings often overshadow logic, so it's best to put
off these discussions until emotions have cooled. Offer to talk about the
issue later, and if your TLO tries to hook you into a discussion while
emotions are still high, calmly and firmly refuse.

Ask for Permission to Comment

An excellent technique for beginning a conversation is to ask permission to say something. You don't need to do this all the time, but if
you fear that your friend or relative may react defensively or angrily to
what you want to bring up, ask her permission. You might say something
like, "Beth, do you mind if I tell you something?" or "Alicia, can I ask
you about something?"

Beginning discussions this way is not a sign of weakness or fear.
Quite the contrary, asking permission is an intelligent and respectful
way to bring up difficult subjects. It has the benefit of making the listener more psychologically open to what you have to say if she gives you
permission to continue.

Your troublesome loved one may say no to your request. Honor
that decision. You'd be acting aggressively if you tried to force her to
talk about a subject she's told you she doesn't want to discuss. Hopefully
she'll be open to talking about the issue later, but she may not, and you
can't do anything about that.

Acknowledge Your Difficult
Loved One

A very effective way to help your TLO stay calm as he's talking is
to acknowledge what he's saying. It's usually as simple as nodding your
head or saying something like, "Yes, I hear you" or "I get it. I get what
you're saying." Speak sincerely and confidently with good eye contact.

This confirms for him that you're listening. Let him take the lead in saying what he wants to say next.

Acknowledgments are an important part of communication and may be used quite frequently. With your acknowledgment, you aren't necessarily saying you agree or disagree. You're acknowledging that he has expressed something and that you've heard it. It's important he knows you heard him.

Stay in the Present

Resist the temptation to bring up past problems. There may be times when you're very hurt about things that have happened, particularly if they were never resolved. However, going back to them simply doesn't help unless you both agree to discuss them in a positive way. If you can't do so, don't go there. If your TLO brings up the past, lead him back to the present. Don't allow him to drag you back there. Instead, calmly and repeatedly let him know you're not going to discuss the past.

Stay on the Subject

Problematic people are often experts at distraction. Consciously or unconsciously, they disrupt discussions by bringing up all kinds of irrelevant issues. Do not be tricked into arguing with them. If you do, you'll be pulled in so many different directions you'll end up furious, defeated, or with no idea what you were trying to say in the first place.

If your TLO continues to change the subject, consider ending the conversation. He may blame you for not listening or not caring (attacking others is a common way crazy-makers manipulate people). End the conversation if you need to, and don't allow him to control you that way.

Use the Broken Record Technique

A wonderful tool for staying in the present and on topic is the broken record technique. With the broken record technique you respond with almost exactly the same words and phrases every time your TLO tries to get you to give in. You keep repeating yourself. Here's a conversation in which a father uses the broken record technique to fend off his son's attempts to manipulate him.

"Dad, I need you to lend me your car because mine just died."

"Son, I'm sorry, but I can't because I need the car for myself."

"But you lent it to Jenny last year, and I need it now."

"I'm sorry, I need the car for myself."

"Dad, you're not listening to me. You obviously love Jenny more."

"I'm sorry. I need the car for myself."

In this example, Dad refuses to get drawn into an argument. His son is willing to hit below the belt to get his dad angry or guilty so he'll give in and say, "Okay, okay, take the car!" But Dad doesn't fall for it. He uses the broken record technique to avoid being dragged into distracting arguments that would wear him down.

Allow Your Difficult Loved One the Last Word

Fighting for the last word reminds me of the game kids play to see who bats first in a sandlot baseball game. Opposing captains hold a bat straight up between them and alternately grip the bat with one hand above the other until one kid reaches the last open spot on top of the bat. He's the winner. But when adults fight to get the last word, there is no winner and no clear prize. In fact, everybody loses.

In some arguments, your angry loved one's last words might be demands that you do what he wants. As long as you don't agree to do what he wants, you lose nothing by letting him have the last word. In fact, it might be very helpful to let him do so. Having the last word gives struggling people a sense of safety in a world they often can't control. Allow your troublesome loved one the last word. He probably needs it more than you do.

YOU ALWAYS HAVE CHOICES

We've encouraged you in this chapter to examine your own thoughts, feelings, and actions when you communicate with others. You've looked at the difference between clamming up, blowing up, and speaking up and have learned about I-messages and seven super suggestions for better communication.

As you finish this chapter, think about how you'll communicate differently with your TLO from now on. If this seems overwhelming, remember you don't have to stay stuck in your old behaviors; you always have choices. In fact, that's the very point of the next chapter. In it you'll examine some of the many choices you have and how you can make them work for you.

6

The Choices Are Yours

Malik and his niece, Quinn, had always been close, so it worried him to see Quinn and her family going downhill. She and her husband, Anthony, had started drinking excessively, and Quinn had become unusually passive. They'd moved a lot and were now living in a rundown place that Quinn insisted was fine. Worried about her, Malik had urged Quinn to join a support group he'd heard about. After a few months of going to the group, Quinn came to Malik and told him she'd started to face some hard facts about herself and had discovered she could do things differently if she wanted.

"Well, Uncle, I'm glad you kept bugging me to go to this group."

"Why's that, Quinn?"

"At first I didn't like it much, but somewhere inside me I knew you were right—something had to change, or my life was just going to get worse and worse. I kind of liked my little world the way it was before I started going to the group. Well, not really all of it—but it was comfortable. Well, maybe not exactly comfortable. Guess I sound kind of crazy, don't I?"

"No, honey, you don't sound crazy to me. You sound like somebody who's doing some good, hard thinking," Malik assured her.

"Yeah, it is hard, but I think things are already getting better at home. Like last week, while I was weeding the garden, Anthony said,

'I want some supper.' Before, I would've gotten up right away and fixed him something to eat. But that day, I just smiled at him and said, 'Well, honey, I'll be starting supper after I'm done weeding this section. It'll be ready about 6:00.' Not mean or anything—I just said it. He looked really surprised, but he just went off to watch some TV. Then the other morning, we both surprised me again! I said to Anthony, 'How about if you make the coffee this morning. I don't feel like getting out of bed yet.' And he did!"

"That's really great, Quinn! I'm proud of you. I was starting to get pretty worried about you guys."

Quinn stared into space for a minute. "I know. I was too, I think. I guess I started to notice I wasn't so happy with some things. Now I'm finding out maybe I can do something about that. I was scared Anthony would walk out or something, but he didn't. We're even talking more now, and I'm getting help with my drinking. It all feels kind of weird, but good, too. I just didn't know I had any choices before."

THE NATURE AND PERCEPTION OF CHOICE

Like Quinn, you've been learning that change is possible. You've read about factors that affect your TLO and yourself and have learned about letting go with love—what it is, how to do it, and how it can help you. You've thought about a lot of information and have explored your own situation and motives. Now, what the heck do you do with all this?

Begin by recognizing that you have choices, and look at the nature of choice, which is that in every minute of every day, you are making choices. You decide what your favorite color is, whether to eat broccoli or carrots, speak loudly or softly, sit or stand, and so on. Choices of this sort feel automatic, while others seem less so. For example, if a little child is running and bumps into you, do you smile or frown at her? That's a choice. When a coworker tells you he can't finish his part of a job on time, it's your choice to respond with patience or anger. No matter how you feel, you can respond to others with a smile or a snarl.

With your TLO, you may not feel you have as much choice due to the intensity of the situation or the closeness of the relationship. Or, maybe you feel uncomfortable with the idea of having and making choices. And even if you welcome the idea with open arms, do you know how to recognize what your options are or how to pick one option over others?

Read about Beau, who felt confused and stuck for years.

Living with my wife for those years was really hard. I never knew what to expect when I walked in the door. Would she be acting normal and happy, or would I find her crying or yelling at the kids? There was no predicting. Sometimes she wouldn't talk to us for days on end. And she could change in seconds. I had no idea what to do or how to do it. I didn't think there was much help for people in our situation back then. Or at least I didn't know where it was or who to ask. We finally split up, which was a relief in some ways, I guess, but it's not really what I wanted.

Several factors contribute to this very common dilemma of feeling stuck. Many people don't know where to turn, or they believe that:

- They have no choices because they must accept whatever life (or God or fate) gives them.

- They aren't smart enough or good enough to choose.

- Nothing will change anyway.

- They have to make "the best" or "the right" choice every time.

- When one person gains, someone else has to lose.

These beliefs can create a great deal of pressure, and they are simply not true. Having choices has nothing to do with how the universe (or God or fate) works. It has nothing to do with your worth or how long a problem has gone on. And no human being can be sure of the best choice every time. And fortunately, it's entirely possible for everyone in a situation to "win" without depriving anyone else.

The nature of choice is that you always have a choice. Even if you have to choose between two options you don't like, you still do have a choice. You decide how to feel, what to think, what to do or not do, and how to do it.

Think of it this way: if someone offered to give you a comfortable but very ugly easy chair, you might think at first that you had just two choices—take it or not. But those aren't your only options. You could refuse the chair; accept the chair and use it (in the basement, if you want); accept it and give it away or sell it; or accept it and then fix it up.

By approaching situations with an open mind and thinking "outside the box," you become aware of many more possibilities than you might have seen before. In any case, it often feels better knowing there's more to a situation than you first thought. The power and opportunity to choose are available to you at every turn.

THE BIG CHOICES

When it comes to the situation with your TLO, you have many choices about how to think, what to do about your feelings, and how to act and speak. Let's take a look at some of the choices you may be facing and consider what you might do about them.

Stay Together or Stay Away . . . or Both?

Some people who care about a difficult person feel like they're running out of options and may think they have only two choices left—stay with that person or stay away. If you have considered this choice, you know it's a painful one indeed.

But before you make that decision, realize you have a variety of options you can consider. These options, which we discuss in the sections below, can help you live more peacefully and successfully with, or without, your TLO. Even if you've never considered closing the door on your loved one, the ideas and techniques in this chapter offer positive choices that will improve how you feel, think, and act. For the moment, though, let's sort through the options mentioned in the heading for this section: staying together, staying away, or a combination of the two.

STAYING AWAY FOR A WHILE OR FOR GOOD

At some point in a difficult relationship, you might decide you've simply had enough and you want out. Many people eventually make this difficult choice when the pain of staying outweighs the pain of ending the relationship. It is rarely an easy choice. But you're doing your best, and perhaps breaking the ties with someone is your best option at a given time. Yet even staying away from your difficult friend or relative can take different forms.

One alternative to permanent disconnection is temporary separation. This term refers not only to marital separation, but to distancing yourself from any loved one. If you have a friend or relative who is seriously troubled, and you feel you've run out of options, you can take a temporary break from that person. Take the following steps to evaluate your situation:

1. *Think* about why you want to do this. Perhaps you're just plain worn out; you have health concerns; you want to consider the relationship from a distance; other life demands are pulling at you; you've almost gone broke; etc.

2. *Consider* what you'll do to get clearer about the problem person and the situation. Will you get counseling, read books, pray, journal, attend a support group, or go on a retreat?

3. *Decide* how much contact, if any, you want to have with your TLO. If you want some contact, decide who can initiate it. How often? For what reasons?

4. *Decide* how long the separation needs to be; it can be any length of time that will allow you to sort things out. You can always change the duration if you choose to.

5. *Decide* whether you're going to present your feelings and ideas to your loved one as a firm decision you've already made, or if you're willing to discuss how the separation will work.

6. *Tell* your TLO your decisions and as much of your plan as you wish. You do not have to explain yourself if you don't want to.

7. *Carry out* your plan. Remember, this is a plan, not a law. But try to stick to it for the most part, to give yourself a chance to adequately think about your situation.

8. *Evaluate* the plan. During and after the separation, think about how you feel, what got better, what got worse. Making a list of pros and cons can help you sort through these new thoughts and feelings. You might also benefit by talking to someone you trust about the situation. If it's possible and helpful, discuss the changes with your TLO.

If you do decide to take a break, use it to rest and to get realistic about the impact your TLO has had on you and others. Allow yourself to enjoy any relief, happiness, peace, and other improvements you experience. Look carefully at your past efforts to help your loved one and try to sort out what was and wasn't actually helpful.

STAYING TOGETHER—SEVERAL VARIATIONS

The choice to stay with your troublesome loved one can be just as difficult as the decision to cut the ties. The questions to ask yourself are similar, but the outcome is different. You might take a break and then decide to hang in there and keep working at it. Or you might never take time away, deciding to stay, period. Neither of these choices is "more right" or "more wrong" than any other. It's simply your choice.

So, you're sticking around. Now what? You still have choices. One choice is to keep on as you have been, relating to your TLO in the usual ways and getting the usual results. Making the decision to leave things as they are is as much your choice as any other option.

Another variation of staying together is to try new approaches to your loved one and to the situation. Perhaps you've learned some new attitudes and ideas from this book or from a friend or counselor. Maybe you just believe there has to be a better way. If you want to, you can find new ways to think about and communicate with the troubling person you love.

WHAT WORKS AND WHAT DOESN'T WITH DIFFICULT PEOPLE

All relationships are influenced by a variety of factors and dynamics, including the closeness of the relationship, how each person sees herself or himself, and how the people communicate. This section will help you understand two important dynamics that may be affecting you and your TLO.

Person vs. Role

Obviously, your problem relative or friend is an individual who lives and breathes. She is no different than any of the acquaintances and strangers you meet every day. She has her own view of the world, her own successes, struggles, hopes, dreams, and fears. If she were a stranger to you, she'd scarcely make a "blip" on the radar of your life. To people who don't know her, she is just a customer, fellow passenger, or faceless stranger.

However, because she is not a stranger to you and is, in fact, close to you, she does register on your personal radar. Because of the relationship you have, she has a role in your life, a function she's expected to fulfill. In chapter 2, you read that some of society's expectations help maintain order. So do the roles people are given and take on. Unfortunately, the same roles that help maintain a predictable order can also restrict the very people who make and fill those roles.

For example, it's very common for the members of a family to expect one another to act in certain ways. Boy children should do this, young women always do that, and old people never do such and such. Although such roles can provide necessary stability, they can also box people into functions, relationships, and expectations that may become prisons for everyone involved.

So where does choice come in? You can choose to see yourself and your loved one differently than you have up to now. Doing so can improve your self-concept and your relationship, thus making it easier to let go with love. This doesn't have to mean pushing your TLO away. It just means that in your mind you think of him as the adult he is, not as your relative or close friend. If you remind yourself that he's a grown man with his own life to live, it's much easier to decrease your expectations of him and to release him to himself and to his own life. This exercise can help you detach from what your difficult friend or relative does.

Imagine you have a neighbor with whom you're on friendly terms. You greet each other when you meet, and sometimes you borrow a tool or a cup of sugar from one another, but that's the extent of your involvement in each other's lives. You discover this neighbor has a serious problem, and you feel badly for him, but you wouldn't dream of telling him what to do about it. You probably wouldn't lose sleep over his situation, either. You might pray for him or offer some neighborly support, but you probably would not become involved in the details of his life.

Pay attention to the feelings you would have about this neighbor. What might you say to him if he started to cry as you were chatting at the end of his driveway? What would you say about him and his situation to others? Write those feelings and comments on the lines below.

_____

_____

_____

Now close your eyes and picture your troubled loved one. Notice where he's sitting or standing—the living room, office, wherever. In your mind's eye, "move him" to a house down the street. Pretend he is the neighbor you just wrote about. Practice thinking about him the same way you did about the neighbor. Picture the distance that exists between your homes and your lives. Notice that this distance does not mean you don't care or hope for the best for him. It simply means you don't become enmeshed in the details of his life.

Acknowledge that it's not your responsibility to fix his problems. Release him to himself or pray for him if you choose. Recognize that sometimes the best way to help is to let people work things out for themselves, just as you're doing in your own life. By detaching to some extent, you won't feel so drained, and if a crisis does come, you'll be in better shape to help.

Rethinking your connection to your TLO in this way is part of learning to let go with love. You have the choice of how you see your relative or friend—as someone you must help no matter what, or as someone separate from you, who has his own choices to make and his own life to live. And you can offer love no matter which choice you make.

Responsibility vs. Blame

Perhaps one of the hardest things you'll do as you learn to let go with love is to decide who is responsible for various aspects of the relationship you're in with your loved one. It can be a tricky business to assign and accept responsibility for what happens. However, sorting this out is necessary if you want to find greater peace, no matter what your TLO is doing or not doing.

First, it's important to be clear about how we are defining responsibility and blame. Responsibility means that adults are in charge of their own thoughts, feelings, and actions. Even someone who is mentally challenged can be responsible for decisions within his abilities. And being responsible for oneself does not mean you must do everything alone or that you're never supposed to make mistakes. It does mean that it's within an adult's power to decide which thoughts, feelings, and actions she will nurture and strengthen.

Imagine you've just glanced at a photo of your TLO on a shelf, and the thought pops into your mind, "She's so stupid." That idea may come unexpectedly, but you still control whether or not you dwell on it, agree with it, and act upon it. That is responsibility—making choices about what you will and will not do about your own feelings, actions, and thoughts.

Blame, on the other hand, springs largely from someone's ideas about what should or should not happen. In chapter 2 you read that blame points a finger at others, or yourself, for causing problems or for not fixing them. Blame looks for a scapegoat to carry the burden of messy situations. Now, as it happens, humans cannot think two thoughts at the same time. So, if you're busy blaming someone for messing up in some way, you can't very well be examining your own thoughts, feelings, and actions to see what you can do to improve your part of things.

When you accept responsibility for your own responses and choices, you're moving forward. You can put your valuable energy into positive solutions, instead of worrying about what somebody should, could, or would have done.

HOW TO DECIDE WHICH CHOICES TO MAKE

It's all well and good to say you have choices about how to feel, think, and act. How, though, can you know which choice is best? In short, you can't. No one can. Someone might have opinions about what's best, but they cannot know any more than you can. You simply do the best you can to sort out the pieces, and then do something. Often, doing almost anything at all is better than staying stuck.

Think about what you've already tried in dealing with your TLO. Notice what has not worked, and then do something quite different the next time. It doesn't make sense to repeat actions that don't work and expect them to give you a different result. Think of it this way: would you continue trying to sit on a chair that has broken every time, even after numerous attempts to repair it? No, of course not. That wouldn't make sense.

The guidelines below will help when you want to deal with your TLO differently. For this example, imagine you're a woman who wants to stop trying to fix her father's life.

1. *Start by listing all your enmeshed behaviors.* Let's say you normally:

   ■ Call in sick for him when he's hungover

   ■ Defend him to others

   ■ Make sure he takes his medication

   ■ Remind him about his appointments

2. *Cross off the behaviors you don't feel ready to change* and work "backwards" to those you do. Doing this leaves a shorter list for you to consider. Let's say you cross off two things you don't feel ready to change.

   - ~~Call in sick for him when he's hung over~~

   - Defend him to others

   - ~~Make sure he takes his medication~~

   - Remind him about his appointments

3. *Narrow your choices to one.* Now narrow the shorter list to one change you're ready to tackle right now. Let's say you decide to stop defending your father to other people.

4. *Think in small steps.* Even the one behavior you decide to focus on can be broken down into small steps. List all the people you usually make excuses to. Then start by not defending him to one person on that list. Maybe you choose your best friend, because you know she'll remind you if you do start defending him. As it gets easier not to defend him, branch out to other people until you rarely, if ever, find yourself defending your father's actions.

Repeat this process for any enmeshed or blaming behaviors you decide to change.

MAKING YOUR CHOICES WORK

Making different choices about how you will relate to your TLO is likely to arouse a full range of emotions in you, including some you might prefer not to feel. How do you handle this part of the change process? The following suggestions will be helpful.

- Give yourself permission to change your mind and feelings. Sometimes, in fact, that's the best thing to do when circumstances or your perceptions change.

- Step back and evaluate once in a while. How's it going? How do you feel? What's helping and what isn't? Talk with someone you trust who will bolster your confidence and give you new ideas to consider. If things don't go the way you thought they would, learn to see that you haven't failed—you've had learning opportunities, and you can choose how to feel about each of them.

- Give yourself credit for your efforts, successes, and learning.

- Let yourself vent sometimes. Write in your journal or let off steam with someone you trust.

You've now read about the nature of choice, some alternatives that can help you deal with a problematic person, and several guidelines to help you make the best choices for you as you learn to let go with love. Now, we'll look at two more approaches that can improve how you relate to your TLO: four words to consider getting rid of, and giving fair warning.

Four Words Worth Losing

The way you think influences the way you talk, and vice versa—changing the way you talk can change your habitual ways of thinking. The four words below are well worth eliminating from your vocabulary, because in most cases they reinforce negative thinking. Instead of focusing on what's wrong with someone, you'll start paying attention to what you like and appreciate about her. Your frame of mind becomes more positive, and your ability to let go with love grows.

ALWAYS AND NEVER

Oh, such inflammatory words! "You always curse and yell!" "You never pick up your clothes." As much as other people's actions can drive you crazy, the reality is that it's almost impossible for anyone to always or never do anything.

One of the simplest improvements you can make in your approach to your TLO is to eliminate the words "always" and "never." Even if you're late quite often, are you *always* late for every appointment? Probably not. Does your partner or friend really *never* show appreciation for your efforts? Not likely. By getting rid of those two little words, your thinking and communicating instantly become more positive and accurate.

TRY

Much of the time, the word "try" carries a buried excuse that can be pulled out if things don't work. "Well, I tried to be more patient, but he's just too frustrating!" or "I've tried to stop paying her fines, but she won't have money for food if I stop." In many cases, using the word "try" implies that the "trier" doesn't have enough power to change. To turn that around, eliminate "try" from your vocabulary and state what you will do or what you expect. For example, "I will stop telling him what to do" rather than "I will *try to* stop telling him what to do." Which statement sounds stronger?

Do you have control over what you say and do? Yes! So take responsibility for your decisions, knowing you don't have to be perfect. *Do* what you've decided to do, don't just try.

SHOULD

This word is loaded with expectations and blame, just as "always" and "never" are. "They should know better than that." "I should've been faster getting dinner on the table." "He should spend more time with his partner." Why? Can one person know what another person "should" do to demonstrate love, be a good mate, or anything else? And even if you were right, would it be helpful to point your finger in blame?

By learning to eliminate "should" from your vocabulary, you free your mind and heart to attend to the facts, let go of judgments, and make your own choices—independent of other people's thoughts, feelings, and actions.

The following exercise will give you a chance to practice decreasing your use of these four "losable" words. Rewrite the following statements without the italicized word. To give you an example, the first statement has been fixed in two different ways.

He *always* tells me what to do.	He tells me what to do really often. OR I don't like it when he tells me what to do.
I'll *never* give you money again.	
I hate the way you *always* yell at me.	
I'm *trying* to be firm with her.	
Please *try* to pick up your clothes from now on.	
He *should* tell me where he's going.	
You *shouldn't* spend your money on things like that.	

On the lines on the next page, in the left-hand column, write some statements you use with your TLO that include "always," "never," "try," and "should." Then in the right-hand column, rewrite those statements in stronger, more positive language.

Rephrasing your own habitual statements is a great way to feel prepared to communicate more successfully with your TLO.

Fair Warning

Sometimes it's very hard to change yourself, and when that change affects others, the challenge increases. Your TLO (and others in your life) might feel uncomfortable or resentful when you change the way you talk and act. And you might feel guilty about "causing" their discomfort. So before you embark on making certain changes, you can give fair warning.

For example, let's say you've been giving your adult brother money every month, even though you resent the fact that he spends a lot of it on the nightlife and expensive clothes. You've had many arguments about his lifestyle and his use of the money you give him.

Now you've decided to change your tune. You see that you've been enmeshed with him. You realize he's perfectly capable of looking after himself because he is an adult. You also acknowledge it's really none of your business how he spends his money, no matter where those spending habits take him or how much you disapprove. As a result, you have decided to decrease your stress by no longer giving him money and by getting off his case about his lifestyle.

With fair warning, you inform your brother of your decisions before you act on them. You can explain how you came to this decision if you want to, but you don't have to. You tell him you're going to learn not to comment on his choices, though you might slip sometimes. You also tell him how the stoppage of money will happen and when. It's up to you whether you stop the checks suddenly or gradually, but with fair warning, you lessen the shock to him and to your relationship with him. Fair warning can also lessen the guilt you might feel about making changes that affect another person.

Remember, even with fair warning, your TLO might be angry with you. But that's not your problem, and it's not within your control. You've given fair warning to help yourself feel better and to give him time to adjust and prepare. It's not your job to ensure he likes the changes.

PRACTICE MAKES BETTER

As you learn to be more conscious and aware of the choices you make, remember that all you can do is choose the best alternatives you can see at any given moment. Accept each decision as being your best right here and right now. The old saying "practice makes perfect" is misleading and sets up an unrealistic expectation. A new saying, "practice makes better," is more helpful, because improvement is certainly possible, while perfection is not.

So, consider your choices from a new angle. No matter what has gone on so far, you are capable and creative enough to look beyond your usual responses. You can learn new skills and approaches and do whatever seems best to you. You can choose to be peaceful rather than passive; silent instead of silenced; self-aware, not selfish; forthright without being critical; and strong rather than rigid. It's your choice.

7

Family and Friends

Healthy family and friends can be tremendous allies when dealing with a troubling loved one. Unfortunately, some troubled loved ones create problems that challenge the skills and patience of even the healthiest families.

In the story that follows, Jim and his daughter talk about Henry—Jim's son and Melanie's brother. Henry, thirty-seven, has two young children with different mothers, has never been married, and is not involved in his children's lives. He's been arrested several times, is chronically unemployed, and disappears from the family for months at a time.

Jim had just gotten a promotion at work and was excited to share the good news with his daughter, but the minute he arrived home she met him at the door and said, "Dad, Henry got arrested again last night. I don't know exactly what happened yet. He made me promise not to tell you, but I've got to tell you."

Jim felt really upset. "Melanie, don't feel bad about telling me. I want you to tell me what's going on," Jim said. "You're my daughter and we've never kept secrets. But the stuff Henry does is just so frustrating! Why do these things always happen when my life is going good? There's never any peace."

"I know, Dad," Melanie replied. "But if Henry finds out I told you he'll be furious. And if I don't tell you, I'll have nobody to talk to about it. I'm in the middle again. I wish I didn't even know what he's into, but I do. I don't want you or Henry mad at me. What am I supposed to do?"

"Melanie, I'm not mad at you. I just get frustrated with Henry when he tells you things and demands you keep them secret. It's bad enough he's in trouble again, but this secret-keeping and game-playing make it a hundred times worse. And your mom will be upset if we don't tell her about it. But if we do tell her she'll go straight to him, and he'll blow up and want to know who told her. Then we'll get into these big fights about who told who—instead of dealing with what he did wrong. I'm so tired of this."

WORKING TOGETHER WITH FAMILY AND FRIENDS

In the example above, Jim and his daughter struggle with their TLO's manipulating ways. They experience fear and anger but ultimately work together by expressing themselves and being honest.

When family and friends are at their best, they communicate honestly and openly with each other. They listen to what other family members have to say. They search for agreement rather than someone to blame, and they all contribute in some way to solving the problems presented to them.

The challenge of working together with family and friends may be great, but you can succeed. This chapter explores ways to do just that. It's worth noting that the concepts and techniques presented here are geared toward loving family and friends, but are equally effective with anyone else.

If you would like your family members to work more closely with each other, you may have to be the one to get the ball rolling. Begin by approaching family or friends who are most likely to support the cooperation you're trying to encourage. Consider starting with one person you particularly trust. Get her support and talk to her about bringing your ideas to others.

Throughout this process, it's usually much more important that you all agree to work together than it is to agree on exactly what to do with your TLO. That is, listening to each other and working cooperatively is a great deal more important than agreeing on details.

Intentional Conversations

Having intentional conversations is one method for working effectively with family and friends. There are two main objectives with intentional conversations.

- To achieve a specific outcome during or after your discussion
- To conduct yourself in a specific way during the conversation

An example of an intentional conversation might be a discussion a husband has with his wife about her giving money to their daughter, who is a TLO. Let's say the wife gives their daughter this money secretly and against his wishes, and previous conversations they've had about this have always ended in arguments.

To stop arguments and create healthy results, try intentional conversations. The first goal of an intentional conversation is to achieve a specific outcome during or after that conversation. There could be any number of outcomes you might want. In this example, a successful outcome might be that the wife would agree to only talk to their daughter about money when her husband is present, or that she'll stop giving her money entirely.

The second objective of conducting yourself in a specific way during the conversation could have one of many desired outcomes. In this example, the person starting the conversation may have the goal of staying calm, or listening more to the other person, or assertively saying what's on his mind.

Note that being intentional in your conversations does not mean you are responsible for how those conversations turn out—or how other people conduct themselves. You have an influence over those things, but you are not responsible for them. You are responsible for how you conduct yourself. And with intentional conversations you decide how that is. The following points will help you carry out intentional conversations.

KNOW YOURSELF

A crucial first step in communicating with others is to know yourself. Examine your own thoughts, feelings, and actions when talking with someone else. The goal of this self-awareness is to know what feelings you have and to work through them rather than be surprised or controlled by them.

UNDERSTAND WHAT OTHERS GO THROUGH

Be aware of the experiences and feelings of other family members. They are usually different than yours. Put yourself in your loved one's shoes. Think about how their experiences with your TLO affect them.

TALK OPENLY

Conflict flourishes in secrecy, so talk openly and often with caring family members. This is a good way to avoid being manipulated by TLOs. Allow all family members to express their views. They may have excellent points you hadn't considered. You might not agree with them all the time, but you can honor their opinions. When you do this they'll be much more likely to work with you.

SHARE INFORMATION ABOUT NEW DEVELOPMENTS

Keep each other informed about new developments in the family. If your TLO has gotten into trouble or has other problems, let close people know. Don't assume they heard the same things you did; in fact, assume they didn't.

Do not confuse sharing information in this way with gossip. Gossip is cruel, unkind chatter that reflects the insecurity and insincerity of the speaker. Appropriate sharing of information is an open, honest process intended to benefit all members of the family.

BE POSITIVE

Talk about what is working in the family more than what isn't. Look for things that are going well and talk about them. It's easy to be negative, particularly if other family members are. But negativity robs you of energy and confidence to solve problems and communicate interactively. So remain as positive as you can.

BE HONEST AND ASSERTIVE

It takes courage to speak up when your honesty goes against what others believe. But communication in your family will go much better in the long run with honesty. Half-truths and little white lies erode trust. Honest and assertive communication causes family members to trust one another and be more open and honest.

BE FLEXIBLE

Be open to new ideas. If a family member has something to say, listen. Don't get stuck in doing it just your way. If you've tried your solution a hundred times and it hasn't worked, open up to the ideas of others. Always maintain firm boundaries to protect yourself from being used or abused by others, but be flexible at the same time.

DON'T JUMP TO CONCLUSIONS

There's an old expression in carpentry that goes, "Measure twice, cut once." Put another way: avoid mistakes by being careful and accurate. If you hear that a TLO or anyone else in the family has gotten in trouble again or been hurt by others, seek more information before you react. Consider the source of the news. Listen to all sides. Gather information and listen carefully before you speak; doing so could prevent a lot of embarrassment and conflict later on.

SUPPORT EACH OTHER

Offer your assistance to family and friends. Ask for their support when you need it. Don't allow differences among family members or your TLO to pull you apart. Stick together and support each other even when you disagree on the details of what to do.

All families face challenges. The healthiest families support each other through those challenges. Your family can, too. Use these principles of intentional conversations in any discussions you have. Take the lead in this, and help your family get closer.

Learn more about your own family dynamics by completing the exercise below. Write phrases that describe the strengths and limitations within yourself and other members of your family. These could include communication styles, personality differences, family loyalties, or anything else that affects family interactions. Write your own sentences after the following three examples. If you think of more, write them in your journal:

Strengths	Limitations
Aunt Sally is a quiet leader.	I can't say no to my brother.
My brother is more open to discussion lately.	My mother and sister haven't talked in years.
I'm learning to stay calmer.	My dad is too suspicious of others.

Strengths	Limitations

Thinking now about just yourself, on the lines below, describe one or two of your most valuable strengths. Then describe how you could use that quality to benefit your family. For example, you might find that one of your strengths is "I am very optimistic," and you might use that strength by deciding that "when my brother starts to cut our sister down, I will bring up positives about her."

_____

_____

_____

On the lines below, describe one limitation you have that could be improved with focused effort. Then write how you will improve on that limitation. For example, a limitation could be "I overreact every time someone brings up my daughter-in-law's name." You could then write how you'll improve on that: "When I hear her name I'll work hard not to make a face, get sarcastic, or try to turn others against her. I know deep down that reacting calmly will help other family members avoid taking sides."

_____

_____

_____

Use the awareness gained from this exercise to change how you interact with others. If it feels safe to do so, share your insight with other family members. Always build upon your strengths and work to improve on limitations.

OVERCOMING BARRIERS BY WORKING TOGETHER

As Jim and Melanie showed us in the opening story of this chapter, troubling loved ones can create havoc in a family. One of the most common ways they do this is by insisting that family members keep secrets about their crazy-making behavior. When secrets are kept, anger and mistrust grow, communication stops, and relationships fracture. This is especially true if family members are already overwhelmed with problems of their own.

It takes insight, communication, and hard work to survive the challenges presented by difficult loved ones. But when your family works together, challenges will be easier to handle. There are many reasons why some family members don't work cooperatively. Some of the more common reasons are:

- They're enmeshed with or disconnected from your TLO.

- There's a history of conflict or mistrust in the family.

- They see the problem and solution differently than you do.

- They get conflicting advice from others.

- They fear the anger of other family members or your TLO.

- They're stuck in old behaviors.

- They see agreement with you as disloyalty to others.

To help clarify which hurdles are the greatest for your family, write your own description of barriers in your family.

_____

_____

_____

Because you can't control what other people do, you probably won't manage to overcome all the obstacles facing your family. But a caring heart, open communication, and healthy decisions will help tremendously.

To overcome barriers to togetherness in your family, always express yourself honestly and respectfully to family members, and stay calm as you do so. Encourage others to express their thoughts and feelings, but don't allow yourself to be dragged into arguments. Use I-messages. Avoid you-messages. Recognize that your goal is not to get your way, prove a point, or be right. It is to work together, build trust, and overcome problems.

COMMUNICATION'S VITAL INGREDIENT: LISTENING

Listening is a basic part of any successful communication. The more your loved ones recognize that you're truly listening—even when you don't agree with them—the more likely they are to be receptive to your ideas.

In the work environment, communication is primarily a method of passing on information to get the job done. Feelings are often secondary, and in fact, are often seen as getting in the way of accomplishing a task. In the family, however, sharing feelings and caring about others is at least as important as getting the job done. In the family, communication isn't just a method of conveying information; it's a tool for creating emotional intimacy.

In chapter 5, we talked about using I-messages to express yourself well. Let's look now at two aspects of *listening* well. One is through your body language. The second is through something called interactive listening. Interactive listening lets your loved ones know you care, and it does even more—it decreases conflict and arguments.

Body Language

Your facial expressions and body movements send a lot of signals to your loved one about how much you're listening. Being very aware of the signals your body sends will help you communicate more clearly. The following behaviors are examples of body language that show you are listening. Learn to use them when a family member talks to you.

- Put down your newspaper, turn off the television, and get rid of other distractions.

- Turn your body to your loved one.

- Look your loved one in the eye.

- Nod your head to show interest.

- Keep your hands still.

- Keep looking at your loved one throughout the conversation.

Interactive Listening

With interactive listening you ... well ... listen interactively. Half of interactive listening is listening carefully for the deeper meaning of your loved one's words, and half of it is responding to what your loved one says with statements that show you're listening.

Your loved one's words may not be accurate expressions of what she actually means, but, rather, clues to the thoughts and feelings beneath her words.

If, for example, your loved one says, "I hate you," understand that her words are affected by her anger. Instead of taking this personally and reacting with your own hurt or anger, stay calm. Respond to your loved one in one of two ways: 1) state back to her what you think she's thinking or feeling, or 2) repeat some of her same words back to her. These responses help her feel understood and accepted. Feeling understood, she's likely to stay calmer and argue less. In this example she's probably angry, so respond interactively simply by saying, "I know you're mad."

Because of her strong emotions at the time, she might say things she doesn't mean. With interactive listening you look beyond her inaccurate words and respond instead to her thoughts or feelings. Don't argue with her about whether she hates you or not and don't overreact by telling her you hate her.

Don't tell her you love her, either. As sincere as your love is, saying so sometimes adds fuel to an angry person's fire. It may seem to her you're trying to be superior—presenting yourself as the perfect loving person while she's out of control. She's too angry to receive your love when her emotions are high. Instead of telling her you hate her or love her, respond with a neutral interactive listening statement.

With interactive listening you respond to your loved one's thoughts and feelings beneath what she says. When you do this you'll steer her into a deeper level of communication. Pick up clues about her thoughts and feelings from her body language and words. Does she seem angry, scared, nervous, hurt, or happy? Imagine what you'd be thinking or feeling if you were in her situation.

When you respond to her, be sure your voice is not mocking, guilt tripping, or sarcastic. Use a neutral tone. You also don't want to sound overly sympathetic or worried. That can come off as weak on one hand, or superior on the other. Show concern, but don't belabor your point. You want her to understand from this conversation that you hear her deeper needs.

The examples below offer ideas of what to say to a loved one who appears upset.

Your Loved One's Words	Interactive Listening Responses
"This is stupid. I'm not doing it!"	"You seem mad right now."
	or
	"I see you're upset."
"I give up. I don't care what you do."	"You sound sad."
	or
	"You seem kind of down right now."
"I hate doing everything for everybody."	"It sounds like you don't think it's fair."
	or
	"You feel like you do all the work."
"I'm sick of being nice. Alberto doesn't listen to me. He never cares what I think."	"You're sick of it."
	or
	"Sounds like you're mad at Alberto."

With interactive listening, allow silence after you speak. It may be difficult to do this at first if you're uncomfortable with silence. Many people think they have to keep the conversation going. But silence is necessary for interactive listening. It gives your loved one time to think and feel.

If your loved one wants to say something back to you, she will. If she doesn't, that's perfectly fine. The silence allows her to be in her thoughts without feeling responsible for answering you. This can help your TLO become calmer.

RESPOND WITH STATEMENTS INSTEAD OF QUESTIONS

You may have noticed that all the responses above have been in the form of statements, not questions. Much of the power of interactive listening lies in this feature. Questions often give your loved one the impression you're quizzing her rather than listening. Your questions may even sound like prying. In any case, questions take her away from her feeling state before she's emotionally ready.

For example, if a loved one seems down and you ask her, "Are you sad?" she gets pulled from a feeling state to a thinking state to answer you. She may not be ready for that yet. On the other hand, your response of "You seem sad" is a simple statement about something you've noticed. It doesn't require an answer. But it does let her know you notice her.

Interactive listening statements are not admissions that you agree with your loved one or that she's right. They simply confirm that she feels or thinks a certain way—and that you are listening. This is very important.

Questions are fine for conversations about what time dinner starts or what your loved one thought of the movie you just watched. But conversations about emotional subjects work best when you use statements rather than questions.

Here's a chance for you to practice using some interactive listening statements. Read the statements in the left-hand column below, and practice saying the interactive listening statements on the right. We've started you off with three completed examples. As you enter your own responses in the remaining examples, remember to use statements that either express what you think your loved one is feeling or thinking, or use statements that contain some of her own words.

Your Loved One's Words	Your Interactive Listening Statement
"I hate it when Sam mocks me!"	"It looks like your feelings are hurt."
"Why should I help Jeanette?"	"You don't want to help Jeanette."
"Virginia will never call me back."	"You seem worried she'll never call you back."

In the next three examples we've done part of the work for you. Finish the sentences on the right.

"I don't give a damn what Mother does."	"You seem_____."
"I refuse to talk to Dad anymore."	"You are really _____ with Dad."
"I hate Uncle Joe. He's so selfish."	"You think Uncle Joe _____."

Complete the following examples on your own.

"Amy is so wicked. She called me a jerk."	_____
"I'm terrified to stand up to my daughter."	_____
"I'm useless. I give up."	_____
"He doesn't care if I live or die."	_____

Keep your interactive listening responses as brief as the examples above. You might think you have to say more, but you don't. These short statements acknowledge your loved one's thoughts and feelings without bringing up additional topics she might argue with. You can use interactive listening several times in a single conversation, and keep each response brief.

Don't be tricked into arguing with your loved one. Hear her words as clues, not facts. Accept that she is upset, and use interactive listening techniques to help her calm herself and feel understood.

FAMILY AND FRIENDS TOGETHER

It isn't always easy to work together with family and friends, but the advantages of doing so are great. Working together makes problems easier to handle and resolves them more quickly. When you work together you get support when you need it, and you feel less alone. When you use intentional conversations and interactive listening techniques, others will be more cooperative with you, and you'll feel more confident in telling your truth.

We move now to a valuable discussion about boundaries, negotiations, and contracts. These are interactive concepts and techniques that will support your continuing work to let go with love.

Boundaries, Negotiations, and Contracts

Tara, thirty-four, had bipolar disorder. Her sister, Jessie, who is twelve years older, had looked after Tara since they were kids—sometimes whether Tara wanted help or not. Tara felt that, despite her illness, she managed her life well. She was smart, had a car and an apartment, and hadn't had any major episodes for quite a while. Recently Tara asked to borrow some money, but Jessie said she would put conditions on any money she lent her.

Tara blew up. "What do you mean, you want to handle my money for me?! I have a job, and I only need two hundred dollars for a few months. Why do you try to control every single thing I do? You don't like it when I go to the movies, you don't think I should buy makeup, you tell me who to date. I haven't had any problems for ages, so what's your problem?"

"Now, Tara, I don't control every single thing you do. I'm just giving you sisterly advice and help. You know you're not always very stable, and you've had money troubles before, so I only want to make sure you don't end up in a bad situation again. If you want me to lend you money, that's how it's going to be. You'll have to give me your bills and your paycheck and let me handle your money from now on."

"Well, that's just stupid! I'm not a little kid anymore, Jessie, but you still think you can run my life. Just because I'm bipolar doesn't make me an idiot, you know. And it doesn't make you my doctor or my banker, either. If you don't want to lend me the money, that's fine. I'll ask somebody else."

Whether you identify with Jessie or Tara, or whether you can see both sides of the story, the relationship between these two sisters leaves room for improvement. Both women have done their best to love the other and to live their lives, but the friction is there nonetheless. They would both benefit greatly by learning to use the tools described in this chapter.

BOUNDARIES, NEGOTIATIONS, AND CONTRACTS

The purpose of this chapter is to tie together some of the skills you've been learning so far. You'll find it easier to communicate, let go with love, and make choices if you're clear about what you do and don't want in your relationship with your troublesome loved one.

Boundaries, negotiations, and contracts have to do with the "rules" of your interactions with any friend or relative. Their purpose is to clarify roles and strengthen relationships, and they may be used in any combination or individually, depending on the situation and the people involved.

A boundary within a relationship is similar to a boundary between two properties: it indicates a limit. Such limits let others know what you will and won't do and what you will and won't accept. These limits are based on your beliefs, abilities, preferences, and choices. The purpose of personal boundaries is to feel better about your interactions with another person, without setting out to hurt that person. There's no right or wrong—only what works for you or what doesn't, within an atmosphere of respect.

Negotiation is a discussion intended to produce an agreement, whether it's between families or nations. Negotiation requires give and take and is based on the idea that both parties (or all parties, if there are more than two) have valid needs, preferences, and choices.

A contract in a personal relationship is usually an informal agreement in which two or more people clearly set down what each person will or will not do. In the rest of this chapter, we'll explain how boundaries, negotiations, and contracts can enhance your relationships.

Boundaries

One struggle many people have with problematic friends and relatives is not knowing how to "shut things off" or "get some space." Personal boundaries can help you feel less "knocked around" by your TLO's crazy-making ways and can convey to others what you will and will not do. Boundaries involve two kinds of standards:

1. What you will or won't do, such as:

   ■ I won't tell lies to cover for my partner.

   ■ If a store clerk gave me too much change, I'd return the extra money.

   ■ Even when my nephew yells at me, I refuse to yell back.

2. What you will or won't accept from others, such as:

   ■ I would say something if a coworker touched me sexually.

   ■ If my neighbors' dog made messes in my yard, I'd speak to them about it.

   ■ When my lover calls me names, I tell her that's not okay, and I leave the room.

You don't have to like or agree with someone else's boundaries, and they don't have to like or agree with yours. Your boundaries are based on your own ideals and a desire to protect yourself from poor treatment. You aren't putting up walls between you and another person; you're simply indicating your limits.

To understand boundaries more fully, consider what not having healthy boundaries is like. People with unhealthy boundaries might:

   ■ say yes when they mean no, or vice versa;

- do things for others that don't feel good;

- feel like a doormat;

- repeatedly defend or explain their choices.

If this list sounds familiar, don't worry—there's a lot you can do to set firm boundaries, beginning with recognizing the ones you already have in place.

WHAT BOUNDARIES DO YOU HAVE NOW?

Everyone has some personal boundaries, though not everyone recognizes them. Perhaps you are unsure about your own boundaries. Or you might find you have clear boundaries with some people or situations, but not with others. Read Susan's story to see how that can be.

I've been working all my life, and at the same time, I love doing things for my family. But over the years, I've found myself doing too much for them, things they could do for themselves. I am always, always there for them, and I'm paying the price. I feel tired and burned out. I've been learning to set boundaries where I work, yet when it comes to my family, I just cave in. Slowly, I'm learning not to say yes all the time, because if I don't take care of me, there won't be any "me" to take care of.

What boundaries have you set? Are some harder to set and maintain than others?

Check off any of the sample boundaries below that apply to you, even once in awhile. In the blank lines, write any other boundaries you've set and that you enforce at least some of the time. Once you complete this exercise, talk with someone or write in your journal about when and with whom your boundaries are hard to maintain—as Susan experienced in the story above.

Boundary	✓
I don't give money to people who can earn their own.	
I don't stick around when people yell at me. I calmly leave the room.	
I say no when I want to.	
I don't make excuses for other people's problems.	
I don't lie.	
I don't finish people's work for them.	
I refuse to buy alcohol for a problem drinker.	

As you did this exercise, you may have found more or fewer boundaries than you thought you had. That's okay, either way. The point is to become more self-aware and to make decisions that serve you. From the examples above and from other boundaries you've identified, consider what new boundaries you want to set up and which existing ones need to be strengthened. Write about your discoveries in your journal. The following section will help you work on your boundaries.

HOW TO CREATE AND STRENGTHEN BOUNDARIES

Now you've thought about the limits you already have, whether any of them need to be strengthened, or if you wish to create new ones. Setting a boundary usually involves changing your thoughts and your actions first. Your feelings will change over time.

Here's how Phil worked through his dilemma and set boundaries so he would feel less frustrated and hurt by his daughter, Holly.

My daughter and her husband have really been keeping their distance from the whole family. I miss them and their kids, and

I often ask them over for holidays or just for a visit. They hardly ever respond, no matter what it is. I don't know what to do.

I guess one answer is to just try not to get so mad. And I could let Holly know what the family is doing without expecting an answer. Maybe instead of invitations, I should just tell her what we're up to and not get caught up in what she does. "We're having Thanksgiving dinner at my house at noon, and we'd love to have you there." Then assume they won't come, and go ahead with our plans. If anybody asks if Holly and her family are coming, I'd just say I don't know. If they do show up, extra plates can be set at the last minute. This won't get rid of all my anger, but it might help.

Phil figured out he wasn't getting positive results from his usual ways. He only felt hurt, angry, and embarrassed—and none of that made his daughter connect any better. Instead, he decided to establish a boundary to deal with her distancing. First, he decided to *think* differently about Holly and her attendance at family gatherings; he stopped expecting her to show up or return phone calls. Then he changed his *behavior* by calmly notifying her once—no more repeated phone calls or angry tirades. Setting this boundary diminished Phil's feeling of being "jerked around" by Holly's silence and absence, and it also helped him let go of some of his hurt and disappointment.

When Phil set the new limits, he had a choice about whether or not he would tell Holly about them. The main point was that the new limits addressed *his* decision to change *his* thinking and actions. This new approach didn't erase all of Phil's hurt feelings, but he certainly felt better than he had before.

Here are three steps you can take to create or strengthen a boundary:

1. Identify the problem situation as well as your feelings, thoughts, and actions regarding it.

2. Decide which of your thoughts and actions you can and will change.

3. Figure out exactly what you will do to replace your old thinking and actions.

Learn to work through the process of setting a boundary by answering the following questions:

What is one situation between my TLO and me about which I don't feel good or in control?

_____

_____

_____

When this situation arises, I usually react with the following feelings, thoughts, and actions:

Feelings: _____

Thoughts: _____

Actions: _____

Which of those are feeling, thoughts, and actions I can *and* will change?

_____

_____

_____

What will I do instead when I start feeling, thinking, and acting in my old way?

_____

_____

_____

This exercise has taken you through the steps of setting a personal boundary. The last statement you wrote is the new boundary. Practice it for a time. Evaluate how it's working for you. You can modify your boundary any time you want, but give it a good try—say a few weeks or months—before you decide it is or isn't helpful. Notice how you feel when you set this limit. If it feels strange, keep it up anyway. Change often feels odd at first, but you will get used to it and, hopefully, grow to like it. If you wish to develop other boundaries, repeat this exercise in your journal or on a separate piece of paper.

Setting boundaries does not ensure that problems will be solved or that all hurt feelings will be fixed. However, boundaries definitely help you gain some measure of control over yourself—the only person you can control. Your TLO might not like the changes you make, but part of setting limits is knowing it's not your job to make everybody happy. It's your job to live your life as well as you can and let others live theirs.

As with all self-care suggested in this book, setting boundaries is not the same as selfishness or unkindness, though it may feel like that at first. Healthy limits simply help you find the energy to enjoy your life and to offer love to others.

Negotiations

As you've been learning, a boundary is one tool that can clarify your position in a relationship or situation. The second tool that aids personal interaction is negotiation, which gives people a chance to work out an agreement together. An underlying principle of negotiation is that both parties have valid views, preferences, and ideas.

A personal negotiation does not have to be a long, complicated process. It's really just a goal-oriented conversation between people who want to improve some aspect of their relationship. (In this chapter, assume the negotiation is going on between two people. More people can certainly negotiate, but that's more complex and might require assistance or greater experience.)

Personal negotiation works best when:

- Both people are willing to discuss the topic at hand

- The topic is specific and concrete

- Neither person has set expectations of what the outcome will be

It's probably obvious from this short list that negotiation will not work with all people or in all situations. However, it is a useful tool that can help iron out tensions between you and your TLO. Let's look at the three points more fully.

BOTH PEOPLE WILLING TO TALK

Negotiation is talk between people who are willing to reach some agreement. For this to happen, you both need to believe it is even the tiniest bit possible to make even the smallest improvement in the stressful situation you share. You both also need to be willing—a small amount of willingness will do—to consider a new approach and listen to one another.

SPECIFIC AND CONCRETE TOPICS

Negotiation works best when you discuss one or two specific and concrete topics at a time, such as when and where you will talk about money or who will cook supper on which nights. It's best to stay away from emotional outbursts, blame, guilt, anger, self-pity, and resentment. Such "emotional ammunition" distracts both people from the specific problem you're working to sort out.

Look at the pairs of statements below. Read and think about each comparison to get a feel for what we mean by "specific and concrete topics" as compared to "emotional ammunition." Which do you think would be more peaceable and effective?

Specific and concrete topic:	When, and under what conditions, you can use my car.
Emotional ammunition:	Why do you always take my car without asking? You're so selfish!
Specific and concrete topic:	How we'll approach making our vacation plans.
Emotional ammunition:	It's so thoughtless of you to refuse, year after year, to plan anything with me.

Specific and concrete topic:	What we'll each do if you end up in jail again.
Emotional ammunition:	I don't understand why you keep stealing! I tried so hard to raise you well.
Specific and concrete topic:	What we'll both do when you lose your temper.
Emotional ammunition:	Why don't you get some help with your anger? You have a serious problem, and I'm sick of it.

Notice that each *specific and concrete topic* statement focuses on both people's specific actions. Discussion of feelings and thoughts is kept to a minimum so the negotiation doesn't get bogged down in the ruts of your history together. The accusations and inflammatory words in the *emotional ammunition* statements create an atmosphere of blame and guilt, neither of which aids cooperation.

Consider Brenda and Don's story. Their adult son, Mike, had been living on the streets for several years. At first they felt terrified, guilty, ashamed, and confused. After a while, they grew angry, too. When he called, they'd try to convince him to come home or get help. Twice they sent money so Mike could take a bus home. Twice, Mike didn't show up. After a while, he called less and less frequently.

With help, Brenda and Don saw that their poor boundaries kept them enmeshed with Mike, and they realized they'd been both blaming him and taking care of him for years—either rigidly laying down the law, or fixing his problems instead of listening to him. Over time, they learned to create boundaries for themselves regarding Mike. When he did eventually call again, they were able to negotiate an agreement with him. Here's how it went.

> When Mike phoned this time, we were ready for him. We told him we weren't sending any more money, and we didn't want to hear his hard luck stories—but that we did want to be in touch with him. If he was willing to talk about what our contacts would be like, we wanted to negotiate with him. We even used those words. We could tell he was surprised—no tears or yelling from us, just a willingness to discuss terms. He didn't want

to talk about it then, but he called back later, and we worked out a few simple "rules" for how and when he would contact us and what we would not discuss. We were surprised at how well it went. Since then, we've heard from Mike twice, and both calls went okay. We feel a bit hopeful now, and definitely more peaceful, whether we hear from him or not.

Don and Brenda had planned what they wanted to negotiate with Mike—if he called and if he was willing to talk. They'd discussed the many difficult issues around Mike's lifestyle and realized they couldn't do anything about his choices or his problems. They could, however, do something about their own feelings by identifying that his phone calls were especially disturbing to them. By planning their hoped-for negotiation around concrete and specific topics, Brenda and Don increased their chances of having positive conversations with their son.

REALISTIC EXPECTATIONS

Having realistic expectations of yourself and others improves virtually any situation—including a negotiation. It's natural to hope for wonderful, positive results when you begin a conversation, and such hope provides valuable "fuel" for your discussion. However, if you let hope blind you to the realities of a person, relationship, or situation, you're not helping yourself or anyone else. A gentle mix of hope and reality often works best.

Brenda and Don had to lower their expectations before they were ready to negotiate anything with Mike. When they first talked about their new boundaries and the hoped-for negotiation, they had several unrealistic expectations. At first they were hoping that:

- Mike would respond to their calmness by coming right home

- No one would get upset

- They would convince Mike to go for drug treatment

- The discussion would go perfectly

Instead, Don and Brenda "did their homework" before they spoke to Mike. They set realistic expectations; were clear about the points they wanted to make; decided not to pressure Mike in any way; and acknowledged that frustration and sadness might arise during their talk with him. After their conversation with Mike, Don and Brenda talked about how it had gone and celebrated the fact that they'd stayed clear and calm.

Contracts

Sometimes you and your TLO need to put a little extra "umph" into your negotiated agreement, and a personal contract can help you do that. A personal contract works more or less the same way a legal contract does—the parties agree to the terms and make the contract binding between them. The personal contract can be written or verbal, and you don't need to use long sentences and fancy language. Just say or write it in your own words. You can even make spur-of-the-moment contracts with yourself.

Some examples of personal contracts are:

- Two friends write up a little contract agreeing they'll exercise together three times a week. They set down the days and times and agree that they won't work out more or less than this amount. The purpose of this contract is to help the friend who is addicted to working out *and* the one who wants to get in better shape.

- A husband and wife are working to improve their marriage, beginning with shared social activities. They agree on the terms they're going to carry out for three months: they'll go out for dinner every other weekend, and they'll join a volleyball team. They mark the dinner nights and the volleyball practices on the calendar and hug to seal the contract.

- A man makes a verbal contract with himself to call his depressed son every Wednesday night for two months.

As you can see, personal contracts can be as formal or informal as you want. The point is to be clear and to agree on the form the contract will take. Here are four steps that will help you create and use effective contracts:

1. Both of you need to agree that a contract will strengthen your negotiated agreement.

2. Decide together:

   - What terms will go into the contract

   - How long the contract will be in effect

   - What will happen if someone doesn't do his part

3. State or write the contract. Sign and date it, or find some other way to commit to it.

4. During and after the contract period, evaluate together how well the contract worked for each of you.

The personal contract gives both of you a chance to (slightly) formalize whatever you've negotiated and agreed to. Make your first contract or two about less stressful topics so you can both get a feel for the process and meet with success. This beginning will lay a solid foundation for future agreements.

PUTTING IT ALL TOGETHER

To recap these three tools for healthier relationships:

Boundaries:

- Are limits set by you, for you, in order to be clearer about what you will and will not do or accept

- Are changeable, if and when you choose

- Improve your ability to negotiate, if you choose to do so

Negotiations:

- Are carried out by you and your TLO together

- Require at least a minimal willingness to work together

- Clear the air regarding specific problems in your relationship

Contracts:

- Are shaped by the topics you and your TLO have negotiated

- Can take any form and contain anything you both agree to

- Help both of you stay on track with your negotiated agreement

Let's look at an example of how boundaries, negotiations, and contracts can work together to improve a relationship. Harold's granddaughter, Becky, has been living with him for the past few years. She suffers from depression, and Harold is happy to help her out, but he's getting tired and frustrated nonetheless. After many ups and down, Harold has come to a decision. He will no longer cook for Becky or remind her to help out around the farm when she's in her "dark days," nor will he pester her if she doesn't do those things. (These are the boundaries he has set.)

When Becky is feeling better, he tells her of his decisions. He tells her how hard it is for him but that he isn't giving up—he just needs to work out a plan with her. They talk together about the challenges and frustrations of her illness. Together, they decide on one topic: that Becky's doctor has stressed the importance of exercise and good nutrition to lessen the effects of depression. Becky and Harold decide together that she has to eat and move around, even when she really doesn't want to. They discuss the details of what she'll do and how often, as well as what Harold will and won't do to help her. (This conversation is the negotiation.)

Lastly, because they both know how disinterested Becky will be when she starts slipping into her dark days, they agree to write and sign a one-month contract—and to make several copies, in case she gets mad and rips them up. Becky agrees she'll make herself read the contract every day for a month, and Harold will put a red star on the calendar for each day she eats and does some form of physical activity. Becky will put up a gold star for every day her grandpa doesn't bug her about eating and helping out. (Even though Becky and Harold are adults, they both like the idea of putting stars on the calendar, because they'll serve as visual reminders of how they're doing with their contract.)

In closing, we invite you to try these three tools for healthier relationships. Fortify yourself with healthy boundaries, which will keep you strong enough to bend without breaking in the winds of your stormy relationship. Then, as you and your TLO decide together, sprinkle your relationship with timely negotiations and contracts. Above all, keep learning about yourself and moving toward greater serenity. In the next chapter, you'll learn about some why's and how's of self-care.

9

"Me" Is Not a Four-Letter Word

Throughout *It's So Hard to Love You*, you've read about finding balance and peace. The surest way to improve the situation with your TLO is to listen to and take care of yourself—first. As you do so, you will experience less stress because you'll know healthy ways to respond to the stressors around you. You'll have tools and ways of thinking to help you move beyond surviving to thriving.

This chapter suggests ways to carry out the second part of letting go with love, which is that taking care of yourself is a loving thing to do that also benefits others. As you experiment with the suggestions for self-care, you'll feel more comfortable in your own skin and will have more control over your life. This is just what the brother and sister in the following story found when they began taking care of themselves and letting go of their other sibling's harmful behavior.

Jenetta and Malcolm had been living in their family home ever since their parents' death several years back. Their younger brother, Terrence, had lived there, too, up until two months ago. After many years of dealing with Terrence's manipulation, lies, and overdependence, Jenetta and Malcolm had finally told him to move out. This wasn't easy for them, and in some ways they felt guilty, but life with Terrence had simply become too overwhelming for them. They were still in contact with Terrence but were learning to change how they related to him. These changes included finding ways to take care of their own needs.

"Well, Jenetta, it's definitely more peaceful around here since Terrence left, don't you think?"

"Yes, but I still miss him. I guess it's just going to take time. Even though I do feel better, I still worry about him sometimes. But I sure do like having time to read and go for walks, without always wondering what he's up to. Sometimes, before he moved out, I felt like I'd just scream if he told me one more outrageous lie! Now, it's easier not to worry about which of his stories are true and which ones aren't. And you know what, Malcolm? It's not just because he's gone—it's because I'm beginning to feel like it's okay to enjoy myself, just because I want to."

"I know what you mean. The other night when the guys asked me to come out for some poker, it felt great to just say yes without feeling like I had to sneak out to get away from Terrence—or take him along. Actually, I think Terrence is the reason I wasn't getting called so much anymore. Now the guys know he's gone, we're talking about a fishing trip. I know they felt kinda bad about leaving me out before, but I can see why they did. Terrence just always seemed to screw things up. Things just feel better now."

Malcolm and Jenetta had different ways of looking after themselves, but the bottom line is that they did it—and reaped the rewards. Their lives became calmer and more predictable, and they had more energy for Terrence when they did spend time with him.

WHAT IS SELF-CARE?

Self-care means doing things that are fun, relaxing, interesting, challenging, peaceful, exciting, revitalizing, and so on. Self-care means doing little things for yourself on a regular basis, as well as making broader changes and creating larger opportunities for yourself.

Whether you already do take care of yourself or rarely allow yourself much downtime to recharge your batteries, it's possible to strengthen your "self-care muscles." Such changes will improve your energy level, emotional stability, and general wellness.

The list below shows some of the changes you might expect to see in yourself and your life when you take better care of yourself. Check the changes you'd like to experience. If you think of other changes you want to experience, list them in your journal.

I would like to ...	✓
Worry less	
Be more relaxed	
Sleep better	
Laugh and smile more	
Feel less stressed	
Have more fun	
Start a new hobby or pick up an old one	
Stop getting headaches, stomachaches, and other pains	
Think more clearly	
Have time for myself	
Spend some money on myself	
Like myself more	
Stop apologizing so much	

These benefits, and many others, can be yours as you learn to pay attention to your own needs and wants more than you do now. Remember, practice makes better. You can get better at saying no to others and yes to yourself.

ME, TAKE CARE OF ME?

The very first step in taking better care of yourself is to recognize and acknowledge that you're hurting. Throughout this book, you've had opportunities to examine your own feelings, thoughts, and actions. We hope you have acknowledged your frustration, pain, disappointment, and other difficult feelings. However, if you still find it difficult to allow yourself to feel shortchanged or hurt, consider the following analogy.

Imagine yourself waking up in the hospital. After a moment, you remember the accident that brought you here and become aware of tremendous pain in your right leg. The attendant reassures you, saying, "You were in an accident, and your leg is broken, but we'll fix you up." It really, really hurts because it's a bad break. But the staff tend to you, and eventually you fall asleep. The next morning, you're awakened by the deep pain in your leg. As you reach for the bell to call the nurse, you notice you now have a roommate, someone who must have come in during the night. The two of you start talking, and you discover your new roommate has badly broken both legs. Does your broken leg suddenly stop hurting because your neighbour has broken two legs? No, your leg still hurts. You might feel grateful your injury isn't as bad as your neighbor's, but yours still hurts, and it still needs to be taken care of.

So when you find yourself doubting whether you "should" feel hurt or if you have the "right" to do something satisfying for yourself, consider the broken leg story. Allow yourself to feel whatever you feel. Life is not a contest to see who has suffered the worst trauma. It's just life, and sometimes life hurts. It's okay to take care of yourself.

TWO BUILDING BLOCKS OF SELF-CARE

To get started taking care of yourself, take a look at these two building blocks of self-care:

1. Willingness

2. Action

Willingness—even the smallest amount—makes it possible to look at new ideas and consider different attitudes about yourself. It means *yes*, or at least *maybe*, rather than *no*. Having glimpsed new possibilities, you'll need to act on them—explore them, see how they feel, find out if they work, experiment with other variations.

Through the use of these two building blocks, you'll discover possibilities and preferences you might not have known were there. You'll see yourself in new ways. Now, let's look more closely at these two building blocks of self-care.

Willingness

If you've been struggling with someone you love, you've probably thought a thousand times, "I'd give anything to make this mess go away," or "I'm so tired of this!" or "I just wish I could make him see." However, wishing a situation would get better is quite different from being willing to do what it takes to change it.

It's natural to wish for and dream about solutions, but such dreams are often vague, unrealistic examples of magical thinking. In chapter 2, you read that magical thinking blocks your ability to focus on what you can and will do to make positive changes. But when you're willing to experiment and work with your own reality, great gifts and wonders will grow. So, look for some willingness beneath your wishes. Ask yourself these "willingness questions":

- Am I willing to consider that I have as much value as other people?

- Am I willing to do something new to help myself feel better?

- Am I willing to feel, or even look, a little foolish while I learn new skills and attitudes?

- Am I willing to discover something new about myself— whether I like what I find or not?

- Am I willing to consider that I have what it takes to improve my own life—even a little?

- Am I willing to succeed? To make mistakes? To accept that my efforts won't be perfect?

If you answered yes to any of these questions, you have enough willingness to grow. If you're even willing to be willing to be willing, that's enough for you to learn to take care of yourself (or to make any change, for that matter).

===

Choose one of the willingness questions from the list above and write your response to it. For example, someone chooses the first question, "Am I willing to consider that I have as much value as other people?" He might respond with, "Sure, I'm willing to consider I have value to my grandkids or my friends, but it's harder to see my value when I think about my nasty brother. I guess I'm open to the idea, if I can figure out how to do it."

Now answer one of the questions for yourself. There's no right or wrong answer—just your truth at this moment. We suggest you ask and answer more of the willingness questions in your journal. Self-knowledge supports self-care, and vice versa.

_____

_____

_____

===

If you don't feel willing to change or help yourself at this time, that's all right. Just keep on reading and asking for help throughout your life, and you will find the answers you seek.

Action

The second building block of self-care is action. When you have a spark (or a roaring fire!) of willingness, and then do something— consider a new idea, give it a shot—neat things happen. You'll feel more confident and relaxed. You'll find you can handle situations that used to confuse and overwhelm you.

For example, Ivan wanted to feel better about himself and do something he enjoyed. Even though he felt shy and unsure, Ivan had a small amount of willingness to risk trying something new. So, despite his own nervousness and the sarcastic comments of his partner, Gary, Ivan attended an introductory writing class. Before and after the class, Ivan reminded himself it was reasonable to take an evening class, no matter what Gary thought. Ivan recognized that if he were going to be happy, he needed to make himself happy. Ivan acted on his little spark of willingness.

If you're willing to pursue a new interest, or look silly, or get rid of negative thinking about yourself, you can. Try that new dance you've been thinking about. Write a positive affirmation every day for a month. Work on your chess game. Relax under the shade of a tree. Whatever you're willing to consider is worth exploring—because you are worth it.

YOU CAN HELP YOURSELF

People in troubling, stressful situations often look outside themselves for relief. They wait for the TLO to change. They want other family members to do more (or less). They eat, drink, work, or sleep too much or too little. They get mad at the authorities for not fixing the problem. If you have looked in such places for relief from your stress, you're probably feeling pretty disappointed and frustrated by now. That's because, as we've said before, you're looking in the wrong places for solutions.

You are the solution to your own worry and chaos. You can rescue yourself. You are capable of finding and using the answers to your own questions. By looking after yourself, you'll renew your spirit, heart, mind, and body. A later section of this chapter discusses external supports, but remember that other people and resources can only work for you when *you* work for you.

As you read our suggestions for self-care, follow your own lead. Listen to your gut instincts. Step around the fear and go for it!

The list below suggests numerous ways you can relax, feel better, get energized—in other words, enjoy yourself. Have your journal and a pen nearby in case you want to make notes. Put yourself in a musing, meandering mood. Sit or lie down in a comfortable place where you won't be distracted for at least fifteen minutes. Slowly read through the list of self-care possibilities, and as you read, notice how you feel about each suggestion. Which ones appeal to you? Which ones don't? Which do you think you might do? Are there some you already do, and is there any way to refresh those activities?

Smile. Giggle. Laugh. Guffaw.

Row a boat or paddle a canoe.

Read something different.

Start a new hobby.

Light some candles.

Take yourself out for ice cream.

Take a rock climbing class.

Play with play dough or clay.

Read to someone.

Take a long bath or shower.

Ask someone to read to you.

Doodle for five minutes.

Watch the stars.

Rock a baby to sleep.

Skip rope.

Brush your hair for five minutes.

Buy or pick flowers for yourself.

Paint with finger paints.

Walk a dog.

Don't answer the phone for a while.

Play catch with somebody.

Hand write a letter.

Howl at the moon.

Read a dictionary.

Bounce a ball for ten minutes.

Build a model plane or car.

Write or read poetry.

Go fishing.

Watch children play.

Be lovingly silent for one day.

Pray in an unusual place.

Do a challenging puzzle.

Make something for yourself.

Join a sports team.

Visit an elderly person.

Dance by yourself.

Do something unexpected for someone.

Slowly walk barefoot across a lawn.

Read one positive affirmation a day.

Color in a coloring book.

Write one positive affirmation a day.

Watch a bug for five minutes.

Walk in the rain.

Listen to music in the dark.

Float on an inner tube for one hour.

Actually smell the coffee.

The number of things you can do to enjoy and care for yourself is infinite. So try some of them! What have you got to lose? (Well, maybe you'll lose a little dignity for a few minutes, but would that be so very bad?)

In the next section, we'll discuss one particular form of self-care—journaling—that has helped many people.

WRITE THIS WAY

In this book's introduction, we explained a little about keeping a journal. Your journal provides a place for you to:

- Experience your own thoughts and feelings

- Explore yourself and your world

- Express yourself

- Expand your awareness and your possibilities

As you've worked through *It's So Hard to Love You*, you have often been encouraged to continue an exercise in your journal. That is one way to use a journal, but there are many other ways, as well. As part of your effort to know and like yourself better, consider these other types of journals and journal exercises:

- *Gratitude journal*—Every day for a month, write five things you're grateful for.

- *Hopes and Dreams journal*—Get those daydreams out of your head and down on paper! Doing so enables you to claim and savor them and, at the same time, makes them more tangible. Once your hopes and dreams have moved outside your head, you're more likely to do something about them.

- *Today's Weather and Main Events journal*—Keeping a daily log of the regular stuff of life is a great way to get started in journaling. It's also a great way to write a history of your life—one day at a time.

- *This week I learned …*—Take time to evaluate your progress in some new endeavor. Give yourself credit and consider new choices or approaches. Think about what worked and what didn't.

- *Right now I feel …*—Get to know yourself better by acknowledging and naming your emotions. Noting your feelings for a while will help you see patterns in your responses to various situations and help you understand yourself more fully.

- *Positive affirmations*—Write the same affirmation five times each day for two weeks. This is a wonderful way to change your thinking for the better and to move forward.

- *Shared journal*—With someone else, write about life, a situation, whatever. Read each other's entries, and respond to one another. Sometimes it's easier to write what you think and feel than to say it. Shared journals are a fun way to enjoy and deepen any relationship.

Though this list of journaling suggestions is short, it gives you an idea of what's possible. In addition to various types of journaling, you can also draw, doodle, paste in pictures or stickers—anything you want that will make your journal an expression of your self.

Use relaxing and interesting pastimes to experience, explore, and express yourself. By expanding your horizons of self-care and growth, you'll be able to reinforce your own strengths and find the answers you're looking for.

OTHERS CAN HELP YOU, TOO

The self-care ideas above will help you listen to yourself and understand what's going on with you. Yet as helpful and necessary as this introspection is, it's not always enough. Sometimes another person's support and guidance really feels good and can help you understand and care for yourself. When you're taking responsibility for your own well-being as best you can, another person and/or resource can help and enrich you further.

The following list describes several types of resources that are helpful:

- *Books, magazines, audiotapes, CDs, Web sites, radio, and television*—Use these to find information, inspiration, and new ideas.

- *Friends and family*—If you feel safe to do so, test the waters with someone close to you to see if he's able to help you cope and grow. Will she listen patiently? Does he have helpful, caring suggestions? Has she been down the "road" you're walking?

- *Self-help groups, support groups, and therapy groups*— Today there are many groups available to help you deal with your struggles, learn new interpersonal skills, and meet people who understand you. Discovering you're not the only one can feel wonderful.

- *Alternative health practices*—In recent years, many people have accepted a number of health and wellness practices that were once considered unusual in North America. Some of these soothing and helpful complementary alternatives are: Reiki, shiatsu, acupuncture, massage, aromatherapy, and chiropractic.

- *Retreats and courses*—Whether it's a meditation retreat or a course in anger management, many communities offer classes and retreat weekends to help you rest, learn, share, and express yourself. Churches, community organizations, colleges, and social service agencies are good places to start looking for what's available in your area.

- *Individual or group counseling*—You can derive great benefit from a professional counselor or therapist. You can expect the following from effective counseling:

  - To feel increasingly comfortable with your counselor and with the idea of counseling

- To gain insight into why you act and feel the way you do

- To gain insight into why others act and feel the way they do

- To acquire tools that will help you deal with your TLO and your situation

- To feel a sense of forward movement for yourself and your life

- *Prescribed medication*—Depending on your situation, a physician or psychiatrist might prescribe medication to help you. Talk with her in detail about why she's suggesting the medication. It is reasonable to expect a professional to fully and clearly explain what she's doing. If you feel unsure about her recommendations, feel free to seek a second opinion.

- *Inpatient care*—In some cases, the best way to help yourself is to check yourself into a hospital or treatment facility. Modern facilities are generally bright, clean, and staffed by caring people who are trained to help. A period of inpatient care can provide a safe time and place for you to receive intensive support and help with the problems that beset you.

The Resources section at the back of this book lists several books and organizations that might be helpful, as well.

GIVE YOURSELF CREDIT

We've mentioned a number of times that it's all right—in fact it's a good idea—to give yourself credit for the progress you make, however small it may seem at times. Just as an Olympic runner began her journey taking baby-sized steps many years before, your journey to greater peace and emotional stability must begin with baby steps, too. You can learn new skills and feel proud for doing so! Read what Marsha said about learning to give herself credit.

I was talking to my friend Sally one night after supper. I was telling her about my great new job at the adult learning center and how scared I felt at first. I told her it wasn't long before I realized how much I enjoyed helping the students. Sally said to me, "Wow, Marsha, you really have a gift. I could never do that kind of work!" I told her it wasn't hard—anybody could do it. Sally stared at me. She said, "No, anybody couldn't do it! I couldn't, and I know other people who couldn't."

The way she said that really hit me. I'd always thought the stuff I did was ordinary—if I could do it, anybody could do it. But maybe not. I said to Sally, "Well, I guess maybe I've been taking myself for granted. And maybe I'd better stop doing that."

Be like Marsha. Give yourself credit for the things you do.

CHANGE BEGINS WITH ME

As you're learning to take care of yourself, you might feel like you're being selfish or going overboard. Such feelings are understandable, but they are not accurate. Helping yourself be strong, healthy, and happy is wonderful. As a bonus, your emerging confidence and calm will benefit the people around you.

So hang in there. New skills require practice, which means doing a skill over and over. You can learn to take care of yourself and take credit for your accomplishments. As time goes on, caring for yourself will feel less strange and more normal. Remember that your choices to love yourself do not deprive anyone else of love—we all have lots to share, and you can do so more freely and peacefully when you love yourself.

10

Growing Forward

This final chapter of *It's So Hard to Love You* ties together information, suggestions, and tools presented throughout the book. The chapter begins with an opening story that shows enmeshed, connected, and disconnected ways of relating to one another. After the story, we'll explain how the story illustrates some aspects of problematic relationships as well as possibilities for letting go with love.

Lily and Ron Mays have an adult daughter, Fiona, and a grandson, ten-year-old Charlie. During Fiona's growing up years, Ron became depressed and grew more distant from the family, while Lily spent a lot of time trying to figure out why he pulled away, though she never really felt she understood it. To compensate for their hurt and confusion, Lily and Fiona created their own unbalanced relationship of caretaking and dependency. In her teenage and young adult years, Fiona began to disconnect in her own way, often taking off for weeks or months without telling her parents where she was. When she did turn up again, Lily would do everything in her power to "help" Fiona sort herself out, while Ron would disconnect as he had in the past.

Once Fiona gave birth to Charlie, the problems escalated further. Fiona went through a postpartum depression that never seemed to lift entirely. Lily became even more enmeshed with her. Over time, Fiona neglected Charlie's emotional needs, though he was usually fed, clothed, and physically safe—often thanks to Lily more than Fiona. In recent years, Fiona had gotten hooked on the Internet, frequently lying to her mother about what was going on with Charlie, the computer, and the men she met online.

Over the years, Ron remained distant and disconnected from Lily and Fiona. Lily often felt that if it weren't for Charlie, she and Ron would have nothing more to talk about than taking out the garbage and paying the bills. She knew it was a blessing for everyone that at least he and Charlie shared a love for cars.

Lily's deep enmeshment with her family over the years had caused her to expend huge amounts of energy trying to keep Ron happy and make Fiona be a better mother. A few years back, Lily nearly had a nervous breakdown, and a friend suggested some books and a support group she thought would help Lily cope with her troubling, troubled, and troublesome family. Since then, Lily has been learning she cannot rescue her loved ones and that it's important for her to look after herself. She's learning not to feel so hurt and frustrated by Ron's distancing and to create clearer boundaries with Fiona. Recently, Lily told Fiona that she expects Fiona to ask her in advance to look after Charlie, not just drop him off at the last minute.

Read what happens when Lily's developing clarity meets up with Fiona's long-standing self-centeredness.

Lily looked up from the book on her lap when she heard Fiona come in the front door, with Charlie right behind her. "Mom, I need you to ... oh, sorry. *Will you* keep Charlie tonight? I'm going out."

"Hi, Fiona," Then smiling and raising a finger to signal Fiona to wait a second, Lily said to her grandson, "And hi, Charlie! How's the model car coming?" Lily reached up to return Charlie's quick hug.

"It's cool, Grandma! I'm almost done. I'll bring it over to show you after I get the decals on it. Where's Grandpa? Working on the Mustang?"

"Yep, but you might want to check out the peanut butter cookies on the counter before you head out to the garage." Charlie barely noticed Lily's smile as he grabbed some cookies and ran back outside. Fiona jumped right in with, "So, Mom, *can* Charlie stay here tonight? I know you told me to give you more notice, but I'm being honest with you. I met a really nice guy online, and I promised I'd meet him tonight.

Charlie could stay and have supper with you, or I could bring him back later. Course, I don't have much in the fridge just now ..."

"Fiona, I really appreciate that you remembered to ask if I'd babysit rather than tell me and that you told me who you're actually meeting instead of pretending it's a girlfriend. But I'm studying for an exam all weekend. I'm sorry, I can't look after Charlie."

"But Mom, this guy is really sweet, and I promised I'd ..."

"Fiona, please don't start telling me all your good reasons. I'm sure your plans are important, but so are mine. I have studying to do, honey. I'm just not available. You shouldn't have promised anybody anything until you checked with me, like I've asked you to do."

"Well, thanks for nothing! I should've known I couldn't count on you. Ever since you started this whole stupid 'Take care of Super-Me' thing, you've turned into a real bitch, Mom. Maybe you can fit me into your busy schedule sometime next frickin' month!"

Lily sighed as Fiona stalked out the door, yelling at Charlie to get in the damn car. Despite Fiona's biting sarcasm, Lily felt good about sticking to her guns. "Well," she muttered, "Good thing they warned me my changes wouldn't always be easy—but they sure are worth it. No more hysterical scenes and nervous breakdowns for me." Picking up a highlighter, Lily got back to her textbook.

The Mays are basically good people who've done their best to show they care and to keep from going crazy. However, until recently, few of their efforts had worked very well.

Take a few moments now to compare your family's situation to the Mays's. Answer the following questions using the story characters' thoughts, feelings, and actions to help you understand your own.

Do you see yourself in any of the characters in this story? If so, who? How are you similar?

_____

_____

_____

Do the characters remind you of your friends or family members? Describe how.

_____

_____

_____

The adult members of the Mays family demonstrated enmeshed, disconnected, and connected behavior, which lead them to use a variety of effective and ineffective communication styles. Look at the table below to see specific examples.

Lily	For many years she was *enmeshed* (trying to make others happy and to fix Fiona's life).
	Then she set clearer *boundaries* and became more *assertive* and *connected* (learning not to be so hurt by Ron's isolating, calmly stating her stance to Fiona, and sticking to her guns).
Ron	For many years he has been *disconnected* (not talking, lots of time in the garage).
	He is, however, somewhat *connected* with Charlie.
Fiona	She grew up feeling hurt and isolated by her father and being overprotected by her mother.
	Later she, too, became *disconnected* (disappearing for long periods, neglecting Charlie's needs).
	She reacts *aggressively* toward her mother and son (yelling and swearing) and has *poor boundaries* (hooks up very quickly with men she barely knows).

Keep in mind that, just like the Mays, most people who love a difficult person (or more than one) face a whole constellation of problems. If this is the case in your life, realize it's normal that even as one problem improves, others might crop up. Continue with the positive changes you're working on, talk to someone, write in your journal. If you're seeing any improvement in your responses to your TLO, rejoice! These improvements will continue if you keep at it.

THE EBB AND FLOW OF HEALING
AND RECOVERY

Everyone's life has a rhythm—even if it's a crazy beat. A disturbing, chaotic life can become familiar. When you change how you think, feel, or act, you're changing that rhythm. Such changes can feel very strange, even when you're the one who initiates the change.

But hang in there. Even if things feel worse for a while, they won't stay that way. You, your circumstances, and your life will improve. The ebb and flow of recovery and change means your life and relationships will move back and forth—happy, less happy; peaceful, chaotic; hopeful, uncertain. But the key is that when you take small steps in a healthier direction, the general trend will be forward rather than backward. You might still cry or rage about your TLO's actions, but as you learn to let go with love, you'll begin to notice you're crying and raging less often and with less vigor. Over time, life will even out for you, regardless of what's going on with the struggling person you love.

As you learn to understand and care for yourself, to improve your communication skills, and to allow your TLO to live his or her own life, you will create more positive events and outcomes—certainly for you, and often for those around you, including your TLO. Letting go with love really works.

Even so, sometimes people and events will crop up that disturb your calm. Minimal feelings of anger, sadness, or frustration can quickly grow into something quite significant. When that happens, step back from the situation as soon as possible. Remind yourself, strongly or gently, to take a few deep breaths. Ask yourself, "What do I want? How do I feel? Do I want to feel angry and sad, or would I rather feel calm and happy? What can I do to feel calm and happy?"

Then do something to help yourself return to a calmer state. Get busy with a task. Solve one problem. Get physically active. Pray. Read or write to sort out your feelings. Take two or three long, slow breaths. Reread the list of self-care suggestions in chapter 9. Whatever you do when problems arise, give yourself credit for any progress you make, and forgive your mistakes.

RAD

As you practice the new skills you've read about in this book, be RAD—realistic, authentic, and determined.

- *Be realistic* about your needs, preferences, and limitations.

  This chapter's opening story doesn't give the background, but Lily would have done some thinking before she told Fiona her new expectations about last-minute demands. Lily's need was to not feel "dumped on" by her daughter. Her preference was to continue helping Fiona, but within Lily's own limitations. And Lily also knew she was not yet able to expect huge changes in herself or her daughter, so she limited her new expectations to something she knew she could ask for and stick to. (This process is discussed in chapter 6, in the section called How to Decide Which Choices to Make.)

- *Be authentic*. Think, dream, muse, and pray about who you are and who you want to be—and act accordingly. What do *you* want? What are your values? What works for you? Then begin doing and being those things. This is authenticity.

  Lily knew she would still love to spend time with Charlie and help her daughter, but she'd been feeling used by Fiona. Her new boundaries allowed her to do what she wanted within more respectful limits.

- *Be determined* to make the changes you decide are realistic and authentic for you.

  Even though Fiona had honored part of Lily's new expectations, Lily still stuck to her guns about wanting to be asked ahead of time. Even if she hadn't been busy with studying, she would not have kept Charlie, because she and Fiona both needed to learn how the new boundaries would work.

As you go along, accept that it's okay to make mistakes. When you learned to drive or cook, did you do it perfectly from the very start?

No, you made mistakes, and you kept on practicing until you were good enough to feel comfortable. The process is pretty much the same with changing your thoughts, feelings, and actions toward a difficult relative or friend.

TWELVE TERRIFIC TIPS FOR LETTING GO WITH LOVE

It's not always easy to let go with love, often because your troublesome loved one has presented challenges that are extremely difficult to handle. You didn't ask for these challenges, but now you must contend with them. The twelve tips presented here will help you successfully deal with those challenges, and live your life in joy, even when your difficult loved one struggles.

1. Let go of the fantasy that you can change someone else.

2. Love yourself.

3. Don't take other people's actions personally.

4. Don't work harder at helping your loved one than he does.

5. Aim for improvement, not perfection.

6. Appreciate small improvements.

7. Remember your own mistakes.

8. Ask for help when you need it.

9. Get your emotional needs met elsewhere.

10. Act "as if."

11. Make your own choices.

12. Decide for yourself what meaning to give life events.

The following explanations will help you understand these twelve tips more fully.

1. Let go of the fantasy that you can change someone else.

You can't change your TLO, regardless of how hard you try, how much you care, or how "right" you are! He might change himself, but you can't change him. Giving up this fantasy is not about letting go of your troublesome loved one. It's about letting go of the idea that you can change someone else.

2. Love yourself.

You might do so much for others that you lose sight of your own needs. If others try to blame you for their mistakes, don't fall for it. Put yourself first more often and take good care of yourself.

3. Don't take other people's actions personally.

Don't blame yourself for your TLO's actions. When you do this you suffer unnecessarily. Her troubling actions are not a sign you did something wrong; they're a symptom of her own poor decision making and a life out of control.

4. Don't work harder at helping your difficult loved one than he does.

Pay attention to who's consistently working hardest on your TLO's problems. If it's you, you're doing too much. Spending more time, money, or energy on your difficult loved one's problems than he does is likely to create emotional burnout in you and overdependency in him.

5. Aim for improvement, not perfection.

Don't pressure yourself or other people to be perfect. Aim instead for meaningful improvement over time. Everyone makes poor decisions, says the wrong thing at times, changes their mind, and feels unsure. Do not punish yourself or others for being imperfect.

6. Appreciate small improvements.

Be very honest with yourself about the change you can expect from your TLO. By definition, troubled loved ones make the same mistakes over and over, so even a small improvement needs to be seen as an encouraging thing. Appreciating small improvements will help you stay optimistic even when the changes are less than you hoped.

7. Remember your own mistakes.

When you get frustrated with your TLO's actions, think back to some of the foolish, irresponsible, or hurtful things you've done. Remind yourself that you turned out okay, and realize that your TLO may also. Do this not to beat yourself up, but to be less judgmental and less afraid for your troublesome loved one.

8. Ask for help when you need it.

Some people are too embarrassed to ask for help, or think they have to do everything themselves. Others don't have healthy people around to give them unconditional support. But going it alone limits your effectiveness with your TLO and adds to your emotional suffering. Ask for assistance freely. Take help that is offered. If you don't have supportive people around you, add people to your life whom you can trust.

9. Get your emotional needs met elsewhere.

Having enjoyable adult relationships and activities recharges your batteries when they are drained by your difficult loved one. Connect with others who are emotionally mature—people you don't have to worry over, take care of, or try to save from themselves. Have fun and stimulating times with these healthy adults.

10. Act "as if."

When talking with your TLO, act "as if" he is listening or cares what you say. Tell him what you think. Don't weaken your message simply because you fear he'll laugh at you or ignore you. Be respectful in how you say it, but tell your truth.

11. Make your own choices.

Decide for yourself what you'll do. Don't allow your troubled loved one, other family members, or anyone else to make your choices for you. Don't let yourself be bullied, guilt-tripped, or manipulated. Listen to others. Try new things. Explore your options. But ultimately, make sure you decide for yourself when you act, how you act, and even if you act.

12. Decide for yourself what meaning to give life events.

Your emotional state stems from your attitude about life. Your happiness is not so much a result of what happens in your life, but how you interpret what happens in your life. Be sure you're the one who gives meaning to your life events, not your troubling loved one, other family members, or anyone else.

LET GO WITH LOVE: PULLING IT ALL TOGETHER

This is not a book about changing others. It's a book about changing yourself. It's important to remember this when you deal with troubling loved ones. When you let go with love you don't let go of your TLO, you let go of trying to control him. You let go of trying to affect the outcome of his actions. You work to accept him for who he is, warts and all, while refusing to let him take advantage of you. When you let go with love, you take care of yourself regardless of what others do, think, or say.

A primary tool for letting go with love is setting boundaries. That means deciding for yourself what you will and will not do for your TLO and what behaviors you will and will not accept from him. By setting clear boundaries, you control how involved you get in your TLO's life. Not having clear boundaries is a sign that you are enmeshed: a state where you identify too closely with your TLO, try too hard, and feel guilty when things go badly. The opposite of being enmeshed is being disconnected. Disconnected people pull away. They cut their difficult loved ones off too much, sometimes completely.

A primary goal of letting go with love is to find the middle ground of connectedness, in which you love your troubling relative or friend, but you love yourself as well. You do what you can to help when it's healthy for you to do so. You keep at least some emotional connection, but at the same time, you do what you have to do to protect yourself from being used or abused.

This leads us to another principle of letting go with love: choice. Your choices may not be easy to make, or even to see, but you do always have choices. When others don't do what you want, you have options of what you'll do next. You choose how you react. You choose how you feel. You do not have to be a victim of other people's actions.

One choice you always have is to be assertive. That means not passively clamming up out of fear or guilt, or aggressively blowing up in anger. It means speaking up and asking for what you want without demanding to get it.

Communication Tools

The communication tools discussed in this book are based on a belief that all people interact with the world through three primary means: thoughts, feelings, and actions. By understanding these three ways of interacting you have a greater ability to know yourself and others, and to make effective decisions.

One very helpful tool for communication is the intentional conversation. With intentional conversations you have two main objectives: to achieve a specific outcome during or after that conversation, and to conduct yourself in a specific way during that conversation.

Interactive listening is another communication technique for letting go with love. With interactive listening you guess at your loved one's thoughts or feelings, or repeat some of her exact words back to her as a statement. A primary goal of interactive listening is to encourage your loved one to express herself by responding to her in statements, not questions. This allows her to feel accepted by you, as it creates trust between you.

You continue communicating effectively by using I-messages rather than you-messages. You-messages tend to blame by focusing on what your TLO did wrong or what you think he has to change. I-messages tell him what's going on with you. They tell him how you feel and what you want. They focus on you, not him, and as a result, he's likely to be less defensive and more likely to respond honestly and openly.

Gaining Insight

Now it's your turn to summarize. We've provided some space below for you to summarize your reactions to the ideas presented in *It's So Hard to Love You*. We invite you to write in your journal if you need more room. First, write about your emotional and intellectual responses to the overall idea of letting go with love. Does the concept of letting go with love make sense to you? Is it realistic? Can it help you with your life? Has it already helped you?

_____

_____

_____

Think now about specific techniques and ideas presented in this book, such as interactive listening, I-messages, choices, boundaries, and so on. Will they be helpful to you? Which ones are you most likely to use in your daily life?

_____

_____

_____

Finally, write one thing you will do differently with each of the following people as a result of your reading this book. Make a commitment to start making these changes very soon.

Myself: _____

_____

My TLO: _____

_____

Other family members: _____

_____

THANK YOU

We hope you've gained a great deal from reading *It's So Hard to Love You*. It takes courage and determination to stay with a book like this, a book that brings up such difficult subjects and raises such powerful emotions. It might seem easier to forget it all and say, "The heck with it. I'm through." But you've stayed with this book and your own learning, which speaks to the love you have for yourself and for that troubled person in your life. You're looking for solutions. We hope we've provided some.

It's been an honor to walk this path with you. You deserve all the credit in the world for hanging in there. We hope you've gained confidence in yourself and have learned practical skills to help you along the way. Even if your TLO cannot or will not change, you can.

We encourage you to keep up the good work. Be assertive about what you want. Connect with loving people. Enjoy your life. Treat all the people in your life with love and respect, and pay particular attention to the only person in the world you can change. You.

✳

Everyone needs encouragement and refreshers once in a while, so we've created two tear-out pages for you. One is the "Twelve Terrific Tips for Letting Go with Love." The other is there to encourage you when the going gets especially tough with your TLO. Feel free to remove them from this book or photocopy them. Keep them where you can easily access them.

Twelve Terrific Tips for Letting Go with Love

1. Let go of the fantasy that you can change someone else.

2. Love yourself.

3. Don't take other people's actions personally.

4. Don't work harder at helping your loved one than he does.

5. Aim for improvement, not perfection.

6. Appreciate small improvements.

7. Remember your own mistakes.

8. Ask for help when you need it.

9. Get your emotional needs met elsewhere.

10. Act "as if."

11. Make your own choices.

12. Decide for yourself what meaning to give life events.

Words of Encouragement When It's Hard to Love

Your life journey with your troubled loved one may well have been a long one. You may have gone through more heartache, pain, and suffering than you ever thought possible. You might be taking this journey with little support from others. You may have wanted to give up many times. And yet you hang in there. You have survived, and now it's time to thrive.

In your struggles you may have found great gifts as well. One gift you can always give yourself is to let go with love. Don't stay enmeshed in your TLO's life, and don't disconnect. Find that middle ground. Stay lovingly connected, while you maintain firm boundaries that don't allow others to use you.

You can continue relating to your troubled loved one as you have in the past, or you can change what you do. One thing is for sure: you will not change your TLO. She may very well change herself, but you can't do it. You can only change you.

Enjoy your life. Live it to the fullest even when others don't. That is your right and your responsibility. Too much sacrifice robs you of your vitality, and that's not good for anybody. You decide what happens in your life, and no one else.

Resources

The resources listed here offer invaluable support, information, and skills that will reinforce and expand upon what you've found in *It's So Hard to Love You*. We encourage you to look into some of these books and organizations.

BOOKS

Beattie, Melody. 1992. *Codependent No More*. Center City, MN: Hazelden. Offers information and help to change one's way of relating to others by learning not to control them and to take care of oneself.

Fisher, Roger, William L. Ury, and Bruce Patton. 1991. *Getting to Yes: Negotiating Agreement Without Giving In*. New York: Penguin Books. Straightforward and positive guide to the basic keys of negotiation at all levels of relationships, from families to corporations and governments.

Gawain, Shakti. 2000. *Developing Intuition: Practical Guidance for Daily Life*. Novato, CA: Nataraj Publishing. How to listen to and develop your intuition or gut feelings.

Guarino, Lois. 1999. *Writing Your Authentic Self*. New York: Dell Publishing. How to use a journal—techniques, tips, and exercises.

Patterson, Kerry, Joseph Grenny, Ron McMillan, and Al Switzler. 2002. *Crucial Conversations: Tools for Talking When Stakes Are High*. New York: McGraw-Hill. Offers skills to help readers carry on positive, productive conversations.

ORGANIZATIONS

2-1-1 Service

Many states in the U.S. and some provinces in Canada have a telephone service called 2-1-1. If your area is serviced, dialing 211 will connect you to an operator who will give you nonemergency information about community services and volunteer opportunities in your area. Services may vary somewhat from one community to another, but in general, you can expect to find information about physical and mental health resources, and support for people with disabilities, elderly people, and families.

> Information: U.S. http://www.211.org
> Canada http://www.211canada.ca

U.S. National Toll-Free Help Lines

The numbers listed on this Web site can be dialed tollfree from anywhere within the United States. These organizations provide mental health information and referrals, and in some cases, crisis counseling.

> www.mentalhealth.samhsa.gov/hotlines

National Institute of Mental Health (NIMH)

The mandate of this American organization is to reduce "the burden of mental illness and behavioral disorders through research on mind, brain, and behavior." On their Web site you will find information about topics such as depression, eating disorders, anxiety, and more, as well as research findings in the field of mental health.

Contact: 6001 Executive Blvd., Room 8184, MSC 9663
Bethesda, MD 20892-9663
(866) 615-6464
www.nimh.nih.gov

Mental Health America

This American organization addresses all aspects of mental health and mental illness. MHA can help you find treatment resources or a mental health professional; learn about medications; research various mental health and family/relationship topics; and more.

Contact: 2000 N. Beauregard Street, 6th Floor
Alexandria, VA 22311
(800) 969-6642
www.mentalhealthamerica.net

Canadian Mental Health Association (CMHA)

This Canadian association "promotes the mental health of all and supports the resilience and recovery of people experiencing mental illness." On this Web site you will find information about emotional wellness and mental illness, as well as where to find a mental health professional or other mental health services.

Contact: 180 Dundas Street West, Suite 2301
Toronto, ON M5G 1Z8
(416) 484-7750
www.cmha.ca

Alcoholics Anonymous (AA)

An international organization for anyone who feels they have a problem with alcohol. Anyone can attend open AA meetings. To join AA, you need only have a desire to stop drinking.

Some of the other programs based on the Twelve Steps of Alcoholics Anonymous are: Narcotics Anonymous, Nicotine Anonymous, Gamblers Anonymous, Eating Addictions Anonymous, and Sex Addicts Anonymous. All these fellowships can be found on the Internet.

Contact: Alcoholics Anonymous World Service Office
Box 459, Grand Central Station
New York, NY 10163
(212) 870-3400
www.aa.org

Al-Anon and Alateen

Affiliated with Alcoholics Anonymous, these international organizations help adults and teens whose lives have been affected by someone else's drinking.

Contact: Al-Anon Family Group Headquarters
1600 Corporate Landing Parkway
Virginia Beach, VA 23454-5617
(757) 563-1600
www.al-anon.alateen.org

Al-Anon Family Group Headquarters
(Canada)
Capital Corporate Centre
9 Antares Drive, Suite 245
Ottawa, ON K2E 7V5
(613) 723-8484
www.al-anon.alateen.org
(888) 425-2666 for information about meetings in Canada and the United States.

Bill Klatte, MSW, LCSW, has been a psychotherapist and social worker for more than thirty-two years. He is currently a psychotherapist with Medical Associates Health Centers near Milwaukee, WI, and has counseled thousands of people individually, in families, and in groups. He gives presentations, workshops, and seminars to professionals as well as laypeople on such topics as parenting, anger management, and self-growth.

Kate Thompson is a writer, educator, life-skills coach, and editor. She has established and operated four social service programs on Manitoulin Island, Ontario, Canada. She is currently teaching courses in life skills and job preparation and is editing a Native studies curriculum. She has facilitated numerous courses and workshops on sexual assault, family violence, abuse, and personal growth.

more real tools for **better interpersonal relationships** from new**harbinger**publications